the little book of
meditation

the little book of
meditation

easy ways to beat stress, improve
well-being, and go with the flow

stephanie brookes

CICO BOOKS

LONDON NEW YORK

This edition published in 2025 by CICO Books
An imprint of Ryland Peters & Small Ltd

20–21 Jockey's Fields   1452 Davis Bugg Road
London WC1R 4BW   Warrenton, NC 27589

www.rylandpeters.com

First published in 2014 as *Meditation Made Easy*

10 9 8 7 6 5 4 3 2 1

A CIP catalog record for this book is available from the Library
of Congress and the British Library.

ISBN: 978-1-80065-428-0

Printed in China

Editor: Elanor Clarke   Art director: Sally Powell
Senior designer: Emily Breen   Head of production: Patricia Harrington
Illustrations: Rosie Scott   Publishing manager: Penny Craig
and Melissa Launay   Publisher: Cindy Richards

Contents

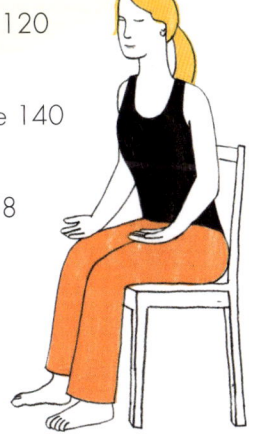

Introduction

A friend first introduced me to meditation in my teenage years. I imagine this was the first "meditative" experience for many of us; it certainly gave us that alternative edge that we so often look for at this particular juncture of our lives. At first, I felt caught up in the mystique of it all—exotic incense permeated the room, well-seasoned meditators all sat in various stages of the lotus position—it was an exciting new experience, yet I wondered, once I had stepped back into the real world, how could it really be of any use?

You may have experienced meditation in the same way and perhaps felt the practice wasn't exactly applicable to your day-to-day life. The image of the Zen-like guru in full lotus position has been weaving its mystical web for so long, the practice itself may seem rather antiquated and not really an essential part of modern living.

Over the years, meditation has come in and out of my life like an old friend; I fall back into a natural pattern within moments of meeting again, yet I have often felt that the hour-long sessions are a bit much for me and that I didn't need "that much meditation" in one go. And so began an overhaul of my routine, a "meditation makeover," if you will. I crafted much smaller, bite-sized sessions, which could realistically fit into my daily schedule, and a routine that actually worked for me. I instantly felt more comfortable and relaxed, with no added pressure.

Our routines have to adapt continually to meet the ever-changing demands of our very real life commitments, and it is natural then that our meditation practice has to readjust accordingly—whether you decide on a daily five minutes, fifteen minutes, or simply integrate mindfulness into your lifestyle—use the practice in the way you want and don't be governed by what the current trend calls for. Meditation has a habit of coming in and out of fashion, but what remains true is that the practice works because it is essentially about cultivating a better understanding of who we are in the here and now. As the world continues to speed up, meditation keeps us grounded in the present, the only place we can ever truly "be."

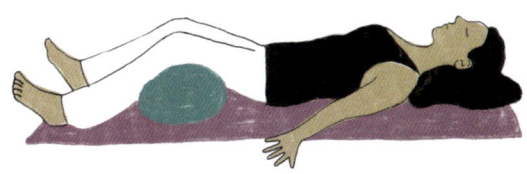

Chapter 1
Why Meditation?

I think the "why" in "why meditation?" is a perfectly valid question, and one that I encourage you to ask. After all, meditation is now a possible addition to your agenda, and how many hours of the day do we have for our own personal and private use? Our schedules are often tough, and the days and years seem to speed up at an incredible rate. It was with this thought in mind that I started to consider how new endeavors are an investment in time and have to be accessible for anyone willing to give them a go. The exercises that I suggest are designed to fit into the most hectic of schedules, so the practice of meditation instantly opens up and not only becomes accessible, but above all approachable. This book will help you get started with meditation right here, right now, so you have the basic tools to start developing your practice. The thing is that you don't have to worry about whether you can fit it in because meditation will bend to fit into your life; it's that simple.

The benefits of meditation

The practice of meditation is already well known for helping with a variety of issues we may be familiar with or have experienced ourselves. For example, meditation helps alleviate stress and anxiety, improves communication issues, helps bring greater clarity to our thoughts and actions, strengthens our concentration, increases self-awareness, and helps us to feel more objective about situations that are troubling to us.

alleviate stress, strengthen concentration, and increase self-awareness

The well-being benefits are enough for anyone to think, "I'll give it a go," but what marks this practice out in a world of ever-changing health fads is the fact that meditation quietly works away in the background, ever reliable, and can be picked up with relative ease, without requiring hours of time or even considerable investment.

Meditation doesn't hand you the answers on a plate; rather, it allows you to come up with the answers for yourself. I have often likened meditation to that friend who just sits with you while you come up with your own answers. You inevitably thank your friend for their help when, in fact, you came up with everything on your own. You just needed that space, that inner sanctuary, to discover what you already knew.

Have a beginner's mindset

The concept of "beginner's mind" originates in Zen Buddhism and was popularized by Shunryu Suzuki in his book *Zen Mind, Beginner's Mind*. Cultivating this way of thinking allows you to approach new experiences free from any predisposed worries, doubts, or uncertainty. Applying a beginner's mindset to these meditation exercises will allow you to simply experience the moment as it unfolds. You may initially experience the pangs of frustration that can overcome a first practice, but just allow yourself to sit with these feelings and observe how they become less and less prominent as you remain firmly in the moment. We are all so used to living our lives at a frenetic pace that, when we consciously choose to slow down, it can be uncomfortable and unfamiliar. One of the key themes we will explore is allowing yourself to feel and to be open to your present emotions, however imperfect they may appear to you. Take your time with this book, and don't feel you need to launch yourself into meditation overload. The meditations are designed for you to dip in and out of and to experiment with so that you can cultivate a realistic and resonant practice. Meditation doesn't require you to be that perfect enlightened being we may have read about in books; it just requires you to be, nothing more.

Time for you

Taking time out for us is often at the very bottom of our to-do list; it may not even be a priority at all. It's far easier to relegate our needs to the bottom rung of importance, and yet it is vital that we do pencil in time for our own needs, even if that means taking a few minutes out of our day just to sit and breathe. Meditation is simply the practice of being in the moment: allowing yourself the time to focus on a singular activity, whether you follow the rhythm and sound of your own breathing, become more aware of your presence and the sensations in your body, or maybe just observe your steps as you take a walk. It is that unique moment in your day when you allow yourself to pause for greater reflection and understanding, which helps calm and de-clutter the mind. We rarely allow ourselves that time and put enormous pressure on ourselves to be "doing" at every moment, be it working ever-longer hours or making sure we keep up with the current trends and fashions so that the outside is looking perfect, leaving little if not any room for our inner life. You could say that meditation is taking care of the "inner business" of living, helping us maintain a good balance between the inner and outer aspects of our lives.

A very brief history of meditation

Meditation has been practiced for thousands of years; its origins span many cultures and traditions, each with their own specific way of practicing. Although the "meditation route" may differ, the end result is the common thread that ties the practice together. The aim is ultimately to find a deeper and clearer understanding of the self.

The most identifiable icon in meditation history is the Buddha; his birth is widely thought to date back as far as 563 BCE. As a young man, Siddhartha (as he was then known) made it his life's purpose to find the cause of man's pain and suffering. After an extensive period of self-discovery, he became enlightened. His subsequent teachings emphasized meditation and, in particular, mindfulness—the act of becoming fully aware of our body, thoughts, and feelings in order to better understand the self—as a central component of his awakening. The beauty of mindfulness meditation is that as much as the roots are in Buddhist tradition, it is practiced secularly and doesn't require any belief system whatsoever. In fact, mindfulness can be integrated at any moment, not just during meditation practice.

If you fast-forward to the present day, the core ideals of meditation have remained—those of compassion, awareness, and a greater understanding of the self—yet the practice isn't confined to a temple or a shrine, but instead can be carried out in the comfort of your own living room. You could say that the practice has traveled far and wide to where it needs to be in people's lives right now.

Misconceptions about meditation

If we can dispel any of the old myths attached to meditation, we can set off in the right frame of mind without any misconceptions, which may limit our knowledge of what the practice can actually do for us. Here are just a few things to bear in mind before you set about your meditative journey.

WHAT MEDITATION IS

A means to help attain greater clarity and focus.

A way to help better integrate you into your life, not take you away from it.

A practice to help you find a greater appreciation of your inner self and life in general.

A quick fix for inner well-being.

A way to escape reality.

An exercise in "who meditates
the best."

Advice from a meditator

After reading this chapter, I would advise progressing on to my suggestions on posture, setting up your meditation space, and so on. However, I know it is tempting to skip to the actual meditation exercises, and this book can indeed be read in a variety of ways. If you have prior experience of the practice, this book may be an aid for further ideas on how to get more variety into your daily meditations, so you may skip to the later chapters. If you are new to meditation, it stands to reason that you will read on to find information on setting up and how to prepare for the meditations to come.

Here are a few little pearls of wisdom I have picked up on my meditative journey to help you get the most out of the experience. Sometimes it really is the little things that make all the difference.

Phone on silent

Cellphones are never far from our fingertips, so you would think that most people would know when and where to leave them on and, more importantly, when to switch them off. I can't think of anything more tiresome than suddenly hearing the latest ringtone echoing loudly around the room. For your meditation session you want as peaceful an environment as possible, not only for yourself, but also if you decide to meditate with a partner or even a group

choose a peaceful
environment and take
a mindful approach to
any distractions

of friends. When I meditate at home, I simply leave my phone in another room to ensure it is out of sight and out of mind. If I am attending a class, I check and then double-check to ensure there will be no embarrassing sounds emanating from my handbag halfway through the session. Cellphones are the ultimate technological temptation, so the quicker this little meditation faux pas is removed, the better. Of course, no conditions will ever be perfect, so if you do hear a cellphone ringing, simply integrate a mindful approach and allow yourself to be aware of the sound without feeling anxious about it.

Comfort is key

Feeling comfortable is vital to the quality of your meditation. If you are in discomfort, just gently alter your position so you are at ease, relaxed, and alert. In the past, I have gone to meditation groups where I have been in discomfort and haven't altered my position for fear I would distract other people, so I have been sitting on an almost dead leg. I don't know what I thought I would get out of the situation, and I felt more stressed leaving the session than on entering, so I quickly learned that moving out of one position and into another was not failing myself or somehow voiding the session entirely, but was in fact taking control and learning to be mindful of my body and discomfort trigger points.

As you begin to meditate, you will soon notice that when your body is at ease, your mind soon follows suit. The mind and body are inextricably linked and the two must work well together if you are to really benefit from your meditative practice. If your mind is racing, your body will be agitated, and if you are physically uncomfortable, you will be unable to quiet your mind. Assuming a comfortable meditation position is of the utmost importance.

Creating your bespoke meditation

Meditation isn't a "one size fits all" practice and can be bespoke to fit your specific needs. You may find, for example, that ten minutes is your meditation "magic number," while for others it may seem too short a time frame, so they would lengthen the session accordingly. There are no rules that apply to a meditation routine; after all, anything too restrictive may feel suffocating, and something that doesn't keep your attention and focus may seem rather superfluous. Finding that meditative balance will instead help you build a session that resonates with you and integrates into your lifestyle.

If you are at the beginning of your meditative journey, I suggest starting with a simple five minutes. In order to monitor your time, keep a watch at your side to track your personalized session. Of course, as you progress, you will get a sense of your timings and will be able to listen to your own internal clock.

Do what feels right for you

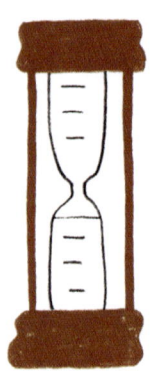

We are all different in terms of what meditation positions, styles, and surroundings work for us. There is no right or wrong way to get the benefits of meditation, it's all about what works and resonates for you. You may find that a seated meditation is not preferable for your needs and lifestyle, so simply adapt your practice to an "on the go" meditation, such as a brisk walk or a run on the treadmill, incorporating a more mindful approach. You can incorporate a meditative practice almost anywhere and at any time. I think there is still a misconception that if you are not in full lotus position you aren't able to reap the benefits of meditation; I would encourage you to throw out the old stereotypes and begin your practice with a clean slate.

Record your practice

It can be useful to chart your own progress by journaling your experiences pre- and post-meditation. The only real barometer of meditation's effectiveness is in the practice, so stay mindful of your progress. It can be particularly helpful to keep a note of your initial time frames; in your journal, write down how long it takes you to prepare for a session, and also jot down any comments about what particular type of meditation works for you. When you're just starting out on your meditation journey, keep a record of all your practice, whether it is five minutes early in the morning or a longer, more relaxed, evening session.

you can practice meditation anywhere and at any time

What helps you get into your meditation "space?"

You may decide, for example, that you need a little background music as you meditate. This is perfectly fine, just as long as it isn't distracting or overly emotive. Try music without lyrics, with the aim of finding something that eases you into the meditation rather than pulling you away from it. Think about the sounds that really resonate with you and make you feel calm and centered. You may also find that you have a ritual that helps you get into the meditation "space," perhaps dedicating a small area of your home to meditation or setting up your chair for such purposes. Make a note of what you enjoy doing and then customize your practice to match your needs.

Which meditation actually works for you?

We are all unique and have completely different meditative needs. As you begin on your meditation journey, start to get a sense for which exercises resonate with you. Don't worry if it takes a while to find the right fit, just enjoy experimenting with the various meditations this book offers and allow the experience to evolve at its own pace.

Your meditation, your experience

As we embark on any new activity, we are likely to already have some background understanding of what it is all about; this is made far easier nowadays with the Internet providing a wealth of information only a few clicks away. We can search through thousands of virtual pages full of advice, facts, histories, essays… The information at our fingertips is positively endless. The one thing we don't get from an Internet search, however, is the ability to form an unbiased, non-judgmental view of our new activity. Internet research ensures we have the opinion of virtually everyone who has ever spoken on the subject. The vast amount of information available to us doesn't stop there, either; we are just as likely to gather opinions from the people around us: "Oh yes, I meditate all the time… This is what happens and the best way to do it is…" or "The only way to meditate is in this position…"

While this mass of opinions is useful and any subject will have innumerable points of view—even this book is coming from my own experiential knowledge of the practice—by cultivating the "beginner's mind" we become open to what the new experience can bring. The beginner's mind gives us freedom as it encourages a willingness to value our own unique perspective and to experience meditation truly in the moment. Acquiring useful information on your chosen subject is well worthwhile, but nothing takes the place of real understanding, which comes from personal experience.

Chapter 2

Meditation, Mindfulness, and Mantra

Meditation is a vast and multi-layered practice; every time you pick up a book or read an article on the subject, new layers of information are peeled back. The practice has its roots in cultures all over the world, so, as you can imagine, there is an extensive list of different styles, each with its own unique philosophy. With this in mind, I have chosen a strand that I feel resonates with us now more than ever and can be practiced with ease and in the comfort of your own home: mindfulness.

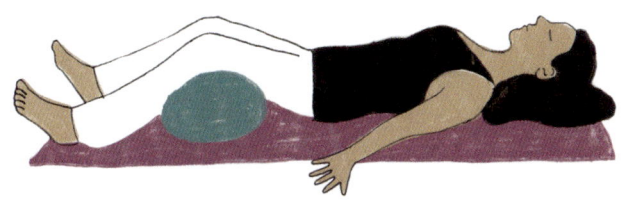

What is mindfulness?

We are always being told to be more mindful, especially in our formative years: mind your manners, mind you don't fall and hurt yourself, mind that glass on the table. I thought the word "mind" went hand in hand with growing up. As we get a little older, we become less inclined to be mindful, and we can often forget as we go about our lives. What I gleaned from my early years was that to be mindful was to become more aware of our actions. I soon learned that mindfulness encompassed all aspects of living. You could say that the moment you commit to living fully in the present is mindfulness in action. It is total awareness of mind and body and observing life as it actually happens. It is being open to the possibility of every changing moment without any form of judgment or criticism; it is "going with the flow" as we might commonly term it. Mindfulness, arguably, is the natural state in which we should all be living.

It sounds so simple, doesn't it—living moment to moment—yet a great deal of our time is spent living anywhere but. We spend a vast amount of our valuable time worrying about events that haven't yet or may never happen or being concerned about a past action that can't be changed. When we become mindful, we begin to notice our lives as they unfold and we start to take note of all the interesting aspects of our lives, whether it be in our

personal relationships, home, or career. With mindfulness, we can start to hone in on our needs and desires, and, conversely, we pick up on what we no longer require on our journey. Mindfulness has a natural association with meditation because you can be mindful and reap the meditative benefits, or you may set about a meditation with mindfulness as the focus.

An expert perspective

I had the opportunity to ask Tonya L. Jacobs, former postdoctoral scholar at the Center for Mind and Brain at the University of California, Davis, about her experience of practicing, and researching meditation. Jacobs co-authored a study showing that there may be a correlation between mindfulness meditation and a reduction in levels of the stress hormone, cortisol. This study was carried out as part of the Shamatha Project, which has received widespread media attention and has also been endorsed by the Dalai Lama. According to Jacobs, if we can train our minds to focus on the present moment, we may be able to reduce the frequency with which we worry about the past or the future, worries that have been linked to an increase in cortisol.

Q: For an individual new to meditation, what, in your opinion, is the most significant reason to start incorporating the practice?
A: In my opinion, a large reason to start incorporating the practice is to become aware of your own thought patterns without getting caught up in these thoughts, as this can lead to destructive rumination and worry. Once a meta-awareness of your thought patterns becomes habitual, you start to have greater clarity as to why you might be feeling certain ways. This, in turn, gives you greater understanding of yourself and others and puts you in better control of your life.

Q: *What are your tips for people who feel they haven't the time or patience even to contemplate meditation? Are there exercises that you think could be useful for the busy individual?*

A: In my experience, attempting to practice at a certain time and in a certain place doesn't work well. However, if I link the practice to something that is already a part of my daily routine, I am much more likely to practice. For example, you can fit in ten minutes of meditation after you brush your teeth every morning. Linking a short practice to my daily evening walks also works well for me.

Mindfulness in everyday life

The beauty of mindfulness is that it can be practiced anywhere, at any time, in all aspects of your daily life. Below are some simple suggestions to help you to incorporate mindfulness into your routine.

The mindful you

This exercise can help you be part of the moment wherever you are; at home, on a bus, or even out and about in the park. In this example, I am basing the meditation on being outdoors.

Find a spot where you can sit comfortably and just become aware of your surroundings. Try to adopt the beginner's mind discussed earlier in this book, which is the practice of looking at experiences with a fresh perspective. You may be surprised that you can use this approach with almost anything; it simply requires a willingness to be present and alert to whatever comes your way. You may, for example, be sat in the park and taking time to observe the trees in front of you; observe them now with a beginner's mind. Notice the beauty, the color, the leaves on their branches or the ground around them, perhaps you notice people as they walk by or even find a spot themselves to take shade—just observe how it appears to you. If your quiet time is interrupted, just accept this distraction rather than struggle with it. If a group of people has distracted your peace it can bring about a feeling of frustration; you may even want to get up to leave, but being mindful of this disturbance can help cultivate an awareness of others, allowing you to adapt

more easily from moment to moment. Life is full of interruptions and disturbances, and it is simply how we respond to these disruptions that helps us form a healthy and balanced frame of mind.

As you get up to leave, keep yourself focused on how you move. You may brush the grass from your clothing, or simply pack up your bag. Remain in a mindful state for as long as you can. You may be surprised by how much more of your day you can remember through continual practice.

Becoming mindful helps us to draw our focus to the present moment and appreciate life in all its forms and qualities. The more you put it into action, the less you will consider it a "practice"—it will just become you living your own life fully.

Become mindful of the little things

This exercise helps us to reconnect with the little things in life that we often take for granted.

To begin, find a place in your home where you feel comfortable enough to sit for several minutes. Take an object of your choice, whether it is an item of jewelry, a flower, a picture, or anything else that you can hold comfortably in your hand. It is best to have an item that is not too heavy or difficult to hold for any length of time.

With your eyes closed, get a sense of how the item feels in your hand. Think about the weight, the texture. Does it feel warm or cool to the touch? Does it have grooves, curves, or pointed edges?

The next stage is to open your eyes and look at the object as if seeing it for the first time. If, for example, you have an item of jewelry in your hand, you may want to examine it closely and get a sense of how the item has been made. Notice the craftsmanship that has gone into creating the item you are now holding. Simply observe the little details about the object, treating it with the interest a child would show.

This exercise shows us how to become more mindful of what is already in our lives; the things we may be aware of peripherally, but simply do not take the time to really see. The idea is to take the principles of mindfulness and apply them where we can to help get more enjoyment out of the little things in life. Next time you visit the park, take the time to look at the flowers or the trees, something of natural beauty, and look at it as if seeing it for the first time. I often use this principle of mindfulness as I travel around the city, whether I'm walking across a bridge or in one of the parks, I make a mental reminder to stop, even if it's just for twenty seconds, to get my bearings and really see what is around me. I know we can't always apply this, and sometimes our surroundings can seem rather dull, but real beauty and interest is all around us. For example, the gadget lover may want to take a moment to appreciate the work that has gone into designing their cellphone, this "can't live without" product, which keeps us in better touch with the people we love and need to communicate with. For the book lover, you may want to look back over the titles you have loved and which have brought you great pleasure over the years, and think about what impact those stories and characters have had on your life. For those who love the outdoors, all you need to do is look up and watch the changing color of the sky, how the clouds drift through it above you. You may not have acres of green fields at your front door, but something that resonates with you will be nearby. Though we can't be presented with the ideal surroundings at all times, we can find the beauty in what is around us, right here and now.

Mindful eating

One of the most enjoyable ways of integrating mindfulness is by bringing it into our culinary lives. Food can become a tool to help us gain greater appreciation for the things we so often take for granted. How often do we actually take the time to think about the way in which we eat? On any given day we are racing against the clock—hastily rushing through breakfast, lunch, and dinner— so food starts to turn into more of a chore than a pleasure. Too often, food only ever becomes something we take the time to enjoy when we are heading to a restaurant or if a friend or partner decides to try out a few new recipes.

Eating mindfully can help you become fully aware of the moment and the real pleasure that food brings to our lives.

When eating mindfully you will notice more easily when you are full, so you are far less likely to overeat. It is when we are fully aware of what we are consuming, and truly present in the act of eating, that we can take greater control over our eating habits.

A MINDFUL EATING EXERCISE

Take a moment to observe your food: what does it actually look like? Is it appetizing? Are you noticing the various textures? What does it smell like? Just spend a few moments with your food and ruminate on these questions. On a busy day we may not even look at what we are about to consume, so take this opportunity to see your food in a new light.

1 As you take your first bite, resist the temptation to eat at your normal pace; even if you are a slow eater, chew even more carefully and get a sense of the variety of textures. What is it you are tasting? Have you picked up on salty, sweet, or sour flavors? Perhaps you have identified an herb or spice you hadn't picked up on before? Is it soft, chewy, or crunchy?

2 Once you have swallowed the food, spend a few moments becoming aware of how this has made you feel. Are you still hungry? Has it sated your appetite? Are you looking forward to your next mouthful?

3 When you have finished your meal, notice how you feel and whether the food has improved your mood and energy levels. Take a moment to cultivate gratitude for what you have eaten.

To conclude: Mindful eating brings our food habits to light. For example, it may be the case that you suddenly realize you haven't been enjoying the food you have been preparing for yourself every day; it's just become habitual. When you start to eat mindfully, you become more acutely aware of your likes and dislikes, and it can be surprising which foods we no longer desire. If you aren't enjoying your food, take the mindful step to change this.

Eating mindfully can also reaffirm just how much you enjoy food and help you feel a greater appreciation for the ingredients you choose and prepare for yourself. For the real foodies out there, mindful eating can help to enrich the culinary experience and heighten the pleasure that food can bring.

A mindful meeting

Mindfulness is more pertinent now than it has ever been. In a world that is increasingly competitive, it is important that we are aware of the moment in which to make our mark and ensure we are heard. In our working life, we can often feel that our opinion isn't valued and sometimes we simply don't have the time to voice our ideas or thoughts. Mindfulness, to that end, can be used very effectively in the workplace with our colleagues, friends, and even potential employers. When we become more mindful we are able to use the moment to our advantage and not let our concerns fall by the wayside. If we are heading to a meeting and want to make the best possible impression, we need to ensure that we are aware and fully in the moment.

It is an unfortunate fact that those meetings that we are most excited or nervous about are some of the places where our thoughts are most likely to scatter into a whole lot of what ifs: What if I say the wrong thing? What if the meeting doesn't go as planned? What if I'm wearing the wrong outfit? It can lead to a flurry of unfocused thoughts that don't have any bearing on what is actually going on in the present moment; we are anticipating outcomes that haven't or may never happen, yet we are letting them control us in the present.

use mindfulness to make
your mark and ensure
that you are heard

TIPS FOR A MINDFUL MEETING

Before a meeting, practice the short mindful breathing meditation (see pages 48–49) to help you calm any scattered thinking or internal chatter—five minutes is all you need.

Remember to switch off your cellphone to prevent seeing any distracting texts or missed calls that may leave you thinking about personal or work-related issues, rather than focusing on the present moment.

During your meeting, allow yourself to really listen and be mindful of the conversation. If we anticipate a question that is asked of us, we often interrupt or accidentally cut off the person's sentence. It's not that we're being deliberately rude, it's just that we have already understood their question and have already formed the response. By being mindful of the discussion, you can adapt to the changing nature of the conversation and also illustrate your strength in listening and communication.

A MINDFUL BREATHING MEDITATION

How often do we really think about our breathing? It is something that occurs so naturally that we don't necessarily have to give much pause to it. In fact, breathing only ever becomes an issue if we find it difficult in some way, then we become far more conscious of what is actually going on. The breath is a central focus for many meditations because it is highly effective at keeping our concentration and helping ground us in the present moment. When we meditate, the first thing we usually notice is the sound of our own breathing. It can be a relaxing experience for some, while others may find it difficult to sit in their own company with just the sound of their breath. It's simply a matter of getting used to the practice.

This exercise is the ultimate go-to for your meditation repertoire; it can be practiced simply and with zero fuss. Try this meditation for five minutes at first and then gradually increase the time you spend on it as you progress.

Follow these steps for more mindful, meditative breathing.

1 In a comfortable seated position, gently close your eyes and bring your focus to the rhythm and sound of your breathing. Don't feel you have to breathe in any special way, just do what comes naturally to you whether it be gentle, sonorous, or heavy; breathe at your own pace and in the way that feels most comfortable.

2 As you relax into the exercise, you may notice that your breathing becomes softer. Now bring your focus to this alteration in rhythm; allow yourself to be present to the ever-changing subtleties.

3 Narrow your focus even further to only the air that touches the tips of your nostrils as you breathe in; it is a gentle observation and one that we rarely experience with such awareness.

4 Focus your attention now on your lips and, as you did with the nostrils, think about the air as it touches the skin. Just be aware of the sensations as they happen and however you experience them. By allowing yourself this level of focus, you quiet your internal chatter, keeping yourself perfectly present and aware of the moment.

To conclude: This breath-focused meditation can be built upon to include further steps (see pages 101–103).

Looking at mantra

We use words every day to communicate our wants and needs to other people, and yet we don't often give pause to how they can be used to nurture our inner lives. In life, it's always best to choose our words with care, and this can also apply to "mantra." Mantra helps us move deeper into the meditative experience; they are used repetitively as a means to still the mind and sharpen our focus. A mantra can be a word, sound, or phrase.

Mantra also acts as a highly effective way of keeping our thoughts anchored in the present moment and helps us to achieve the much sought-after "inner stillness." It is especially useful at the start of your meditation journey as the use of mantra can give you a very specific point of focus.

The ideal word or sound will be soft and easy to say; if the mantra you have chosen feels too clunky or difficult to speak aloud, this may cause a stumbling block in your meditation. It is also important to bear in mind that we are all different, and what works for one person may not necessarily work for another, so experiment until you find your mantra match.

Choosing a personal mantra

We can expand what we think of as a mantra and create our own soothing sounds that suit our unique needs. Words resonate with us in a very personal way, and how we respond to words and sounds differs from person to person. If you have decided to opt for your own unique mantra, choose words or affirmations that don't bring up any strong feelings or reactions. The name of a partner or loved one, for example, will bring up very specific emotions attached to that person, which ultimately ends up being far too distracting. Instead, try to think of a mantra as a blank canvas, a part of your meditation routine that need not be attached to any one thing, place, or person.

Creating your bespoke mantra helps you to put your own stamp on the practice. To get started, follow these simple steps:

1. Gently breathe in.

2. On the exhale, sound your chosen word in rhythm with the breath, elongating it for as long as feels comfortable.

3. Repeat the mantra several times, or for as long as you wish, to suit your personal needs. You may want to incorporate a mindful breathing exercise to round off the meditation.

Many people choose a two-syllable mantra, but if you are just starting to get familiar with the practice, repeating a single word on the exhale is a great starting point. If you decide to use a two-syllable mantra, simply think the first syllable to yourself as you inhale and, when you exhale, you can choose to say the second syllable aloud, or silently to yourself.

THE "OM" EXERCISE

It is important to mention "OM," otherwise known as the ultimate mantra go-to. You have likely heard this mantra before. It is perhaps the most recognizable of all the mantra and is an excellent starting point if you would like mantra to form part of your practice.

Mantra-based practice can be integrated in your meditation routine as and when you choose. Below is a short exercise to get you to grips with OM in no time.

1 Find a comfortable location in which to sit. Place your hands on your knees or allow them to nestle softly in your lap.

2 For the first few moments, just become aware of your body as you relax; notice how your breathing becomes softer as your mind and body become calmer.

3 Bring your attention now to your mouth. Start to move your lips and mouth "A, E, I, O, U" out loud to help the jaw relax and loosen. Repeat this a few times and you will be ready to move on to the next step.

4 Keep your focus as you gently open your mouth to sound the mantra, OM. Elongate the sound so that you are extending the mantra for as long as it feels comfortable. You will feel the mantra vibrate between your lips and inside your mouth. Simply fade out the OM when you feel you need to take your next breath.

5 As you sound the OM, imbue it with power from within and don't be afraid to really give the word some punch; it will resonate better if you sound it with conviction. At first it can sound a little unusual but, over time and with practice, it can be an empowering aid to your meditation.

6 Once you have come to the end of your first OM, continue to recite the mantra as many times as you want; you could try five OMs to begin with. Once you have come to the end, integrate a simple, mindful meditation such as the breathing exercise (see pages 48–49) for the remaining part of your session. The beauty of the mantra is that you can mix and match with other meditations to create an entirely bespoke session.

Chapter 3

Meditation Basics

Experimentation is important when you first begin setting up your "at home" meditation practice. I have outlined ideas on positioning, both seated and on the floor, and I have suggested some equipment that you may need to ensure a comfortable and stress-free practice. All of the ideas are designed to provide simplicity and convenience, so you can work with what you already have at home, as well as integrate further equipment if you feel it is needed. The key is to discover what really works for you, so that meditation can be easily incorporated into your daily schedule. The beauty of meditating at home is that you can get started with minimal fuss. I have laid out the foundations to enable a comfortable and undisturbed practice. Let's get started.

Getting the basics right

One of the key factors of a successful and stress-free meditation has to be comfort. I couldn't even conceive of a worthwhile and beneficial meditation without it. Isn't life challenging enough without having to go through a meditation without optimum support and a sense of ease? I have always believed that if your foot has lapsed into a coma, it's time to make some adjustments. Discomfort will not help you become a better meditator, it will just very quickly dissuade you from the practice, and rightly so; who wants to spend 5–10 minutes every day actively making themselves uncomfortable? Getting into the right position will help still the body and therefore quiet the mind, so you will be able to navigate a successful meditation.

Meditation is also one of those blissful times in the day when your sartorial efforts are not required. In fact, dressing up in order to meditate rather defeats the purpose. If you are "actively" meditating (i.e. taking a seated position in which to calm the body and still the mind), any clothing that feels heavy or restrictive will do little to persuade you to sit still for any length of time. Of course, this slightly alters when you are out and about, but if you are sitting for a meditation, allow yourself to relinquish the nine-to-five look for something more relaxing.

Helpful hint

Make sure you stay hydrated. Before you start any meditation, ensure that you have a glass or bottle of water within arm's reach and take a sip as soon as the session has finished. This allows you to ground after the practice and helps you to readjust when the session is over.

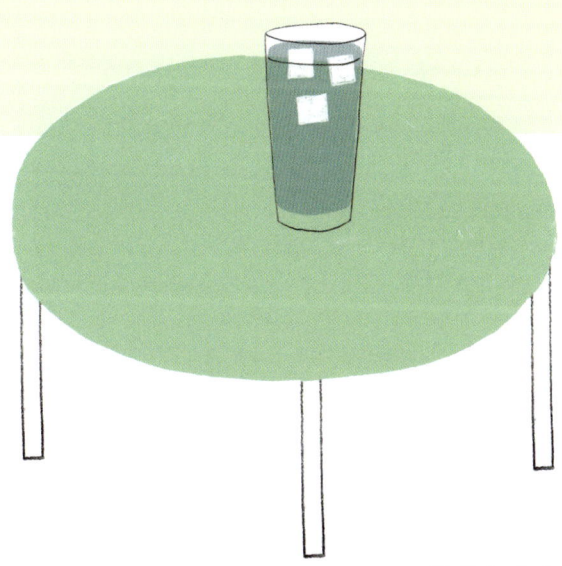

Creating your meditation space

Designating your own little meditation nook will help you create a routine you are more likely to stick to. Simply decide on a place in your home that feels comfortable. All you need is an area big enough for you to sit comfortably so roommates/partners need not worry about their space being taken over! Many of our daily tasks are made easier when they have their assigned home; just think, if we kept moving our toothbrush from the bathroom, we would be more likely to forget or just not bother to brush our teeth on occasion, whereas keeping it in the same place, within easy reach, ensures that we brush our teeth every morning and night. I am not suggesting your meditation routine be this stringent, but however often you practice, assigning a meditation spot that you will return to again and again will make things easier. Give yourself a visual reminder of your space, it can be as simple as leaving a cushion or a blanket there. If you decide that you want a little extra, you can start to create a proper meditation space, designed to be that perfect little oasis of calm, just for you.

You could create a focal point for your meditation practice with a small table, for example, decorated with your personal items and trinkets, however much feels right for you. Choosing items that help

Helpful hint

Socks and a blanket are the meditator's essential tools of the trade. You can often feel chilly during periods of stillness, and you may find that you become aware of even the slightest draft that has managed to find its way into your space, so ensure you stay warm with soft, comfortable blankets and socks.

you to focus and give you a sense of calm is always a good idea. You may decide that you want one focal point, for example, a candle placed in the center. A candle can be used as part of your practice, as shown in the guided meditation in chapter 4 (see pages 114–115).

You can also place pictures, postcards, or inspirational quotes around your meditation area; this is the perfect opportunity to use those items that bring back pleasant memories. It is best to refrain from having items that are highly emotive. If you have a picture of a group of friends and it happens to contain an image of an ex-partner, it's not likely to bring about that perfect feeling of tranquility. I would suggest far gentler images that always have the effect of making you feel balanced and centered. The overall aim of the table, or whatever you choose to use as a central point, is to be a focus for your meditation. A lovely way to put your stamp on this space is to create something for it, whether you write a poem, find a beautiful passage from your favorite book to display, or, if you have crafty fingers, make a small blanket or cloth on which to place all your items.

Once you have finished your meditation, you can leave the space as it is and create a little feature of it, or, if you want it to be more personal, you can conceal your items with a blanket or sheet you like. If you don't have the space to do this, simply place the items in a box, ready for your next practice. This shouldn't be seen as a problem or a hindrance, because the very act of creating your meditation space can become your ritual for getting into the right frame of mind. Rituals can be anything from a few quick breathing exercises to lighting a candle, playing music, or creating your own personalized space.

As you will already have worked out from what you have read in this book, meditation can be as simple or extravagant as you see fit, so you can start to modify your practice however you choose.

Are you sitting comfortably?

For the correct upright position, you should have your back straight and shoulders relaxed. It can help to imagine a cord attached to the top of your crown. Visualize the cord gently correcting your position so it is upright, but not stiff. The aim is to stay alert and focused throughout the meditation.

At the start of your practice, choose a position and location that feels natural and comfortable for you. The obvious first choice might be the couch or a chair; both offer comfort and support and are a great option for seated meditations.

If you decide you want something more "down to earth," and you prefer sitting on the floor, there are a variety of different positions to choose from. Just remember, you should sit in a way that feels comfortable for you. Although the lotus position offers a certain challenge, a simple cross-legged position is equally beneficial for meditation purposes.

To Lotus or not to Lotus?

That is "the" question on every meditator's lips! You place yourself atop your meditation cushion, and, as you begin to assume your position, you get the inevitable "should I or shouldn't I?" feeling. It is best to do what feels right for you; it really is as simple as that. Over the years, I have tried various positions but the two that work best for me are either half lotus or a simple cross-legged position. Remember that meditation is not a contest in who has the bendiest legs, so it is important that the position you choose offers ease and comfort so that an effective meditation can be carried out.

Cross-Legged

The "go to" position if you prefer to meditate on the floor. It is simple, effective, and is commonly used for meditation purposes.

Half Lotus

If you decide that you want to explore a new position, the half lotus is the natural progression. In your cross-legged position, lift one foot and place it atop the top half of the opposite leg, so it is resting on the inner part of the thigh.

Full Lotus position

Only attempt this position if it feels comfortable for you to do so. In your cross-legged position, gently place the right foot so it is resting on top of the left thigh (close to the hip) and place the left foot so it is resting on the top of the right thigh (close to the hip).

Further ideas

Hard-backed chair

If the chair has armrests all the better, because this position will ensure you stay upright, alert, and supported. Also, remember to keep your feet firmly on the ground. You may find that the addition of a small cushion under your feet aids your comfort, as well as one placed behind your back so you feel comfortably supported in the chair. Just experiment with the chairs you have at home until you find one that feels particularly conducive to your meditation purposes.

Lying on your back

To ensure that you are not putting pressure on your lower back, you might like to put a cushion under your knees, especially if you are lying on a hard surface. You can even bend the knees slightly, which again releases any pressure. Also, have a spare cushion on standby in case you need one under your head, and a blanket in case you get cold. This position is most effective for the Body Scan Meditation (pages 107–109).

Whatever you choose, just keep in mind that any position should feel comfortable and stable. If you are perched on the edge of your chair or couch, you will be too unstable; likewise, if you have curled up in your favorite comfy chair, chances are you will drift off to sleep. A good balance between all three—stability, comfort, and awareness—will help prepare you for the meditation to come.

Hand placement

What should you do with your hands? Well, this little conundrum is very simple: what feels comfortable for you? If you are in a seated position, whether on a chair or a cushion on the floor, you will likely naturally place your hands either on your knees or nestle them in your lap. If you decide you prefer your hands on your knees, why not try palms facing up one day, and then palms facing down the next; experiment until you find what works for you.

Eyes open or shut?

It is common practice to keep the eyes half open and softly gaze upon a specific point just in front of you to help you stay in the present moment. If your eyes are partially open, you might like to choose one of the mandalas used throughout the text and focus on it as you meditate. This is, of course, optional; some people find mandalas distracting but for others they can provide a useful focal point. If you keep your eyes closed, it is ideal to have a point of focus to stop your mind drifting off. Your breath is a simple thing to use as an anchor to keep you aware and in the moment, but different anchors may work better for different individuals, or for each different meditation.

Meditation equipment

Over time, you may want to invest in meditation equipment to support your practice further. Below is a list of some popular items, all of which have their benefits. However, what is right for one person may not necessarily be of optimum comfort for you, so keep to what works best for you, rather than letting the current trends or the latest must-have item dictate to you.

MEDITATION WEDGE

The wedge, which works as a cushion, offers good all-around support and encourages a natural upright position. The wedge itself is also compact, so an ideal item if you have limited space.

ZAFU

This firm, plump cushion is ideal to keep you slightly raised off the floor, giving added support for your meditation session. Similar to the wedge, the zafu encourages an upright position. You can tilt your pelvis forward so you are comfortably perched on the edge. This will encourage you to keep your back straight and remain more alert as you meditate.

MEDITATION STOOL

The stool is ideal for meditators who may find sitting directly on the floor uncomfortable. In a kneeling position, you sit on the small seat with your legs tucked underneath the stool itself. Your back will be perfectly aligned and upright.

Alternatively, you can also use household items such as the cushions from your couch, pillows from your bed, or simply a thick blanket folded up and used to rest upon. For extra comfort, you may want to prop yourself up by your bed or couch to help you remain upright. The key thing is to experiment with different positions and also locations within your home to find the place and position that works best for you.

Getting used to the silence

On any given day, if you count how much time you spend in total silence, you are likely to come back with a rather prompt answer: none. I'm talking about those moments where we are in full awareness: the phone is on silent mode, the television turned off, and all you can hear is the sound of your own breathing. Today, try making a note of when you experience true silence and for how long. Silence is a rarity for most of us, especially if you live in urban areas and are never too far from the hustle and bustle. Silence can often seem a little unnerving as it can also bring to light those issues, worries, and fears we all keep hidden. We can get pretty adept at keeping those issues under the surface by drowning them out with a continual stream of noise and activity. With practice, we can get used to our own company, unhindered by life's distractions.

"FEEL" THE SILENCE

There are ways in which we can start to further appreciate moments of peace and solitude. At first, silence may feel uncomfortable, simply because it's not often we allow ourselves time in our day to just "be" without any type of distraction. The trick is not to plunge yourself into a self-appointed solitary retreat; just allow yourself five minutes of uninterrupted quiet time and see how you go from there. Try these suggestions for stress-free silence.

1 Find a time when your home is free from family/friends and simply turn off your cellphone. Remember to pre-empt any possible interruptions; this is your time.

2 Rather than sitting in silence, which can be uncomfortable to begin with, simply wander around your home and take in your surroundings. If, like me, you have an apartment and don't have a huge amount of space, make use of where you can go and pause to take in what is around you—wander about your kitchen, look in the cabinets, peruse the books on your shelf—become mindful of where you live.

3 Keep at a gentle pace and don't feel the need to rush; this is your time to enjoy a little peace, without the need for words, sounds, music, or distractions of any kind.

4 Notice how you feel as you walk around the space: does the silence feel strange? Or does it feel comfortable? As you consider these questions, try not to analyze them, just accept the way you are feeling. There is no right or wrong reaction; it is simply the way you feel.

5 You may find that your initial reaction changes over the course of the five minutes. Whatever feelings arose during this time, it can be useful to keep a journal and simply note down the change. Perhaps the silence was comfortable at first and then became slightly less so, or maybe the exercise highlighted your need for some quiet personal time.

To conclude: This exercise can be carried out at any time you feel you need to press pause and just experience a little mindful time for yourself.

The "soft-core" approach

The long-suffering meditator should take a much-needed exhale when I suggest that meditation need not take hours of your day and can fit into a much more manageable and realistic time frame. Meditation should not make you feel like a martyr, but rather be a practice you can use in whichever way you feel is appropriate. When taking up any new activity, there is a tendency to jump in with both feet in order to tackle our newly chosen path with gusto. This is admirable, certainly, but realistic… Perhaps not. Personally, I have never taken the "hard-core" approach to meditation and have worked with a routine that is in balance with the other aspects of my life.

I like to call these shorter, bite-sized bursts of meditation the "soft-core" approach, as they very gently bring the practice into our daily lives. A lengthy session can often feel a little daunting and inconvenient for most schedules. The soft-core approach is not about cutting corners or skipping any crucial meditation moments; it is simply about being honest about the realities of day-to-day life. We are all pressed for time, and those blissful moments, whether they are five minutes, ten minutes, or longer, are just as worthwhile and helpful to our well-being as more extensive sessions. Meditation, after all, shouldn't take you away from life; it should integrate into the one you are living right now.

Just as there is no ideal meditation length, there is also no such thing as the right time to meditate. The morning is certainly one of the optimum times, but that may not fit in with your schedule. The reality of twenty-first-century living is that we have incredibly varied and busy schedules; someone who starts work at 5am probably won't feel like waking up at 3:45am to fit in their meditation. Likewise, if your evenings are scheduled to the hilt, your lunch hour may be your one opportunity. The following pages offer my suggestions for optimum meditation at morning, noon, or night.

As an early riser, you will have the benefits of undisturbed meditation. Below are some of the reasons for integrating an early A.M. session.

You are relaxed and already predisposed to the meditative state.

Your mind is yet to be cluttered by the stresses of the day.

You are less likely to be interrupted by phone calls and emails as the demands of the day have yet to begin.

THE MIDDAY MEDITATOR

Lunch hours are often spent catching up on emails and phone calls and hastily rushing through lunch before the next item on the agenda. You can, however, use your break for a very speedy session.

It acts as a midday break and can help you to navigate the rest of your day calmly and with more focus.

It is a constructive use of your time, particularly if your evenings are busy or mornings are not an option.

You can choose to meditate with
a friend or colleague and enjoy the
benefits of meditating with others.

At the end of the day, you may find there is more opportunity for personal time and therefore a chance to unwind properly.

You can spend more time creating a meditation ritual and so extend your meditation period to suit your personal needs.

You will feel calmer and less stressed as you unwind from the activity of the day.

You can realistically factor in a practice by assigning yourself 5–10 minutes before you go to sleep.

Thought pop-ups

It is inevitable that a thought or two will pop into your mind as you meditate. The thoughts could be anything from an issue at work to a telephone conversation with a friend, or even a deadline that is continually triggering worrying thoughts. The answer to this issue is quite simple: the mind wanders; it is perfectly natural and human. Of course, some people will naturally possess greater focus to block out internal mutterings, while others may find stillness and focus quite difficult to achieve, whereas most of us will fall somewhere in between these two.

Be adaptable

The key thing here is to be kind to yourself and to restrain your inner critic. Meditation calls for a willingness to adapt to the varying stimuli, both inner and outer, which can come up during the session. It is inevitable that the mind will allow errant thoughts to come up, as if deliberately trying to test your patience. Your scattered thoughts may also be triggered by external events such as a person calling across the street or the low hum of a cellphone that wasn't switched off. Start to integrate these perceived distractions into the meditation, rather than letting them shake you out of your session, by simply accepting that they are around. Equally, be open to adapting as soon as that particular stimulus has made its exit. It can be useful to acknowledge these thoughts because, like any distraction, once the thought or need has been met, it often has little or no more power over us.

Best laid plans

So, you have found your meditation spot, arranged yourself into a comfortable position, the room has gone quiet, and all you can hear is the sound of your own breath. For that moment, you feel a resounding sense of peace; you have managed the near impossible—to actually sit still for a moment and be at one with yourself—no mean feat, I can tell you! But then the inevitable happens; you start to feel the gentle prickling sensation of an itch or, even worse, pins and needles. This can often sound the death knell to a meditation session as the overarching urge to move your leg around as if it doesn't belong to you takes over.

Go with the flow

I have been there, in many uncomfortable ways. I have cramped, itched, forcibly hit my leg to wake it up, and all during a single meditation session. These concerns need not be a hindrance to meditation, though. In fact, they can become the optimum time for you to respond to what your body is telling you, and if you are in discomfort, you can change your position at any time. When I first set out on my meditation journey, I naively thought that the conditions had to be perfect at every moment; if I heard someone padding across the room above I would have to stop… If I felt a breeze I would be distracted… I started to realize that these were all my doing and ways for me to sabotage my own experience. Even in classes, you can often hear a variety of potentially distracting noises; the door swinging open and shut from the floor below, the buzzing of a cellphone that was left on, or someone in the meditation session having a coughing fit—it happens—so I have come to the sometimes uncomfortable conclusion that there will never be that perfect time to meditate. Simply allow yourself to adapt to the moment, as it happens.

Chapter 4
Meditations for Self-Healing

The beauty of these meditations is that you can mix and match them at any given time depending on your mood and needs. For example, when we feel unfocused and agitated we need to integrate mindfulness to refocus and help calm any scattered thinking; if we are feeling in a more reflective mood and have been mulling over a personal issue, we can use our inherent visualization ability to start to work through the problem. The meditations are all designed within a 5–10 minute time frame. The beauty of the shorter time frames is that they allow the practice of meditation to be accessible to all, no matter how busy or pressed for time. Of course, there will be those days when a mere ten minutes seems like an enviable chunk of the day, however, it is likely that a 5–10 minute meditation can be worked into your daily schedule most of the time.

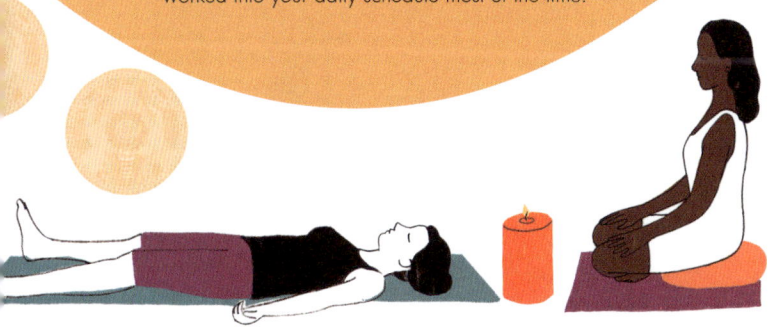

Visualization for meditation

In the following meditations, our visualization ability is brought to the forefront. The following exercise will illustrate how we can easily paint a picture in our minds and bring it to life in our own unique way—so, if you think you lack the imagination to visualize, think again.

I have practiced this visualization exercise alone and also in group sessions, and I have to say it works every time.

Assume a comfortable position at a time and place where you won't be disturbed.

Now imagine that you have just entered your kitchen and are reaching for a piece of fruit in your larder or bowl. Visualize yourself picking up a citrus fruit such as a lime or lemon.

In your mind, take a moment to smell the fruit, feel the waxy, dimpled skin, and enjoy its fresh, clean scent.

Take a knife and cut the fruit in half…See the spray burst from the fruit as it is sliced in two. Then take a piece of the fruit and bite into it, experiencing the tart, sweet juice.

In this visual, you may find that your taste buds are positively tingling and your mouth is salivating, as if you had actually experienced the eating of the fruit. It just goes to show how effective visualization can be and how very simply we can bring a thought to life with color, texture, and, in this case, flavor.

The self-healing meditations

Though the whole idea of "self-healing" can sound a little new age, and doesn't quite fit in with the mood of the modern time— we are all meant to be so fiercely competitive for success, surely this introspection will make us all soft and stop us doing what we need to get to the top?

The fact is that we require greater

self-love

self-worth

self-appreciation

or however else you want to term it, now more than ever before.

We are exposed to such a multitude of technologies and have access to a far greater online and digital presence, but what about our actual, real-life presence? Sometimes our realities can become a little blurred, so while we all need to continually adapt to our fast-moving society, we also need to remember who we are at the core, allowing our sense of self to remain strong and intact.

"JUST AS YOU ARE" MEDITATION

This meditation is simple, unfussy, and can be carried out easily wherever you happen to be.

1 In a comfortable seated position, bring your attention to your breath and follow the gentle rhythm of your breathing. To begin, have your hands nestled in your lap or resting on your knees.

2 Next, put your hand on your chest and notice how it rises and falls as you inhale and exhale. Finally, gently close your eyes.

3 Think about how your skin feels under the palm of your hand, is it warm or cool to the touch? Get a sense of how this simple hand gesture has now changed the course of your meditation as you become more aware of the present moment.

4 You can choose to keep your hand on your chest; however, you may want to bring your hand back to its initial placement, whether nestled in your lap or placed on your knee.

5 Focus now on how your clothes feel against your skin: are they soft and loose, allowing greater freedom in the meditation, or do they feel more restrictive? Are you wearing jewelry? Or a watch? Think about the weight of them and how they feel against your skin; really narrow your awareness to how your body is feeling in this very moment.

6 Now get a sense of how you currently feel in the space you occupy: have you chosen a comfortable spot? Are you in a corner or in a more central part of the room? Are you warm or have you noticed a draft? Begin to expand your awareness to the room around you and your presence within the space.

7 For the next step, expand your awareness to what is happening outside the room: can you hear sounds beyond the room? Can you discern family/friends in the home? Can you detect the footsteps and chatter from passersby?

8 If at any point during your meditation you feel your mind wandering, simply bring yourself back to awareness of your breath. If you notice a thought pop up has entered your mind, acknowledge it: "I am aware that you are there." This can be more useful than simply shutting down the thought and, once you have made this stance, you dissolve any internal struggle.

9 Your breath is a great way of bringing your thoughts back to the present moment, however, if you feel an action is required you can choose a hand gesture, such as placing a hand on the chest (as in Step 2), which instantly brings you back to the meditation.

10 As you continue through the meditation, become aware of your emotions. Simply acknowledge whatever feelings occur and resist the temptation to react to them or analyze them. Allow yourself to be in the moment.

11 Focus your attention back to the rise and fall of your chest and the rhythm of your breathing. Once you feel ready to finish your meditation, gently open your eyes.

To conclude: This meditation is all about a willingness to be in the moment and experience whatever comes your way. Make sure you have a glass of water at the ready to ensure you stay hydrated.

"COUNT THE BREATH" MEDITATION

This is another classic "go to" exercise to add to your repertoire. This meditation always comes up in classes or on courses because of its simplicity and its ability to create a sense of calm by narrowing the focus to counting the breath. Follow the counts to help create a relaxing meditation session.

1 Allow yourself to settle into a comfortable seated position. I would suggest closing your eyes for this exercise so you can narrow your focus even further.

2 At this point, it is not necessary to include the counting step, just keep your focus on your breathing. Allow yourself this level of focus until you start to feel calm and settled. If at any point you feel distracted, just allow whatever you pick up to integrate gently into your meditation—do your best not to feel unsettled by this.

3 As soon as you reach the moment where you feel calm and connected—and by this I mean you have put yourself first—"you" have become the central focus, progress to the "counting" step.

be guided by what you feel is right—put yourself first

4 As you exhale, count the number "one" in your head. You can communicate the number audibly if you so choose. If you decide to do it this way, allow the word to be soft, calm, and spoken in time and rhythm with your exhalation. As soon as you have counted the first number, continue all the way through to the number ten. Once you have reached this number, simply go back to number one and begin the process again.

5 The repetitive nature of this meditation is the key to this exercise. Once we focus on the "count" we narrow our attention even further, as we not only have the sensation of the breath as a focus, but the number does double duty for `sour concentration.

To conclude: This meditation need not be any longer in length than any of the other meditations I suggest. Be guided by what you feel is right and always keep in mind that it is not about the quantity—the quality of the meditation is of utmost importance.

"SELF-APPRECIATION" MEDITATION

This meditation can be used when we need a little more self-appreciation, but it is also a powerful declaration of acceptance and a nurturing exercise. Our self-inflicted criticisms can have adverse effects on our confidence, leaving us with a negative and wholly inaccurate self-image. We always tend to affirm what we consider to be our worst attributes and little if any attention is given to the positive aspects of who we are. Work this meditation in when you feel an unnatural balance in your self-acceptance.

1 Arrange yourself into your preferred meditation position so you feel comfortable and relaxed. You can sit on the floor, propped up by cushions, or you may feel more supported in a chair or on the sofa.

2 Imagine you are sat opposite an image of yourself, aligning with the wiser, more thoughtful aspect of who you are—that is not to say you are not that person already, it's just that so much of our time is spent on self-criticism that we have to remember to see ourselves with greater empathy.

3 Visualize yourself being watched with compassion and acceptance. There is no judgment here or criticism of any kind, just a simple acknowledgment of the person you are.

4 Think about your qualities and what you most appreciate and value. Affirm to yourself that you are perfect as you are, requiring no changes, adjustments, or tweaks; you are the best version of you. Be firm and strong on this point—of course we all have our inner list of things we would like to alter, we are human after all—but we must learn to love who we are in the now.

5 Once you have made your positive affirmation, spend a few moments focusing on your breath.

6 End the meditation by accepting to take small steps to integrate a more compassionate attitude into your day-to-day life. If a friend or colleague pays you a compliment, for instance, don't dismiss it with a self-deprecating remark; simply thank them and acknowledge the compliment.

see yourself being
watched with
compassion and
acceptance

"BODY SCAN" MEDITATION

The following meditation brings the body into clear focus as you quite literally "scan" it to become directly aware of what you are experiencing.

The most common position for this meditation is to lie flat on the floor, with the support of a yoga mat. I would advise using a cushion under your knees to take any pressure off your back and one to support your neck gently. Also, you should keep a blanket nearby as lying still for ten minutes or so, you might get a little cold.

If you don't feel comfortable lying on your back, this meditation can be carried out in the comfort of a chair or couch, just as long as your feet are flat on the ground.

1 Spend the first few moments getting comfortable. Arms should be by either side of your body, with your hands touching the floor.

2 Quietly settle by just becoming aware of the natural rhythm of your breathing.

3 Ensure you are relaxing every part of your body. To do this we use a "clench and release" method by tensing the muscles in the body: clench your hands in fists, clench your toes, stomach, buttocks, and all areas of your body, then release, allowing your entire body to relax into the floor.

4 Just spend a few minutes becoming aware of your body softening so that every part is relaxed and stress-free. Observe how your newfound relaxed state makes you feel: perhaps this is the first time you have felt truly calm all day? Or it might prompt you to realize how much tension you were carrying in your body.

5 Start at the tip of your toes and begin to work through the various points in your body: how do your feet and ankles feel? Notice any sensations that immediately spring to mind, gently working up through your calves, knees, and upper thighs; spend a moment here to relax the legs and feet deeply.

6 Working your way up further still, until you reach your pelvic area, bring your focus here to ensure you are not tensing or holding any stress. As you work your way up to your stomach allow the belly to feel soft.

7 Bring your attention to your arms and hands; you may want to give your fingers a little wriggle just as a way of helping you connect with the meditation and to anchor your focus.

8 As you bring your awareness to your chest area, notice how it rises and falls with the rhythm of your breathing. Has it become softer over the course of the meditation? Are you comfortable as you lie on the floor? If at any point you do notice any discomfort, simply adjust your position accordingly.

9 Observe your head and neck, and remember to relax your shoulders, too. Spend a few moments focusing on the whole of your body, being fully mindful and present in your experience.

To conclude: This meditation is an opportunity to think about the body in a more observant way, and to remind ourselves to be continually mindful of our well-being.

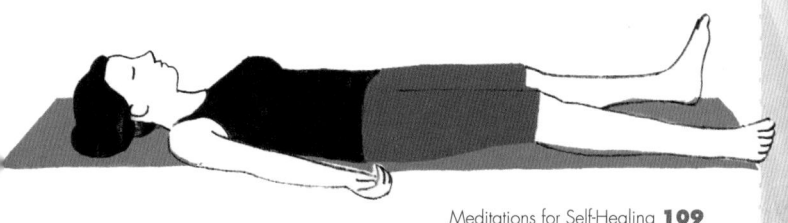

"INNER SMILE" MEDITATION

This meditation stems from an ancient Taoist practice; it is a joyful exercise with the power to uplift and create an inner and outer smile.

I imagine we have all experienced those days where some random passerby feels the need to inject a "cheer up" or "smile, it's not that bad" comment as you cross paths. If we lose our smile, our whole demeanor can often come across as slightly unapproachable. If you carry yourself with a sense of joy, it is infectious to those around you, because you are not only reflecting a demonstrable smile but an inner smile, which radiates from within. It may sound a little odd at first but it actually works in practice; when we feel a sense of happiness and joy we carry ourselves with confidence. We gravitate to people who radiate this smile and we try and avoid those who don't. A genuine smile can resonate from a place deep within.

The great thing about this meditation is that we are guided by the visualization and also by the act of smiling, so we come out of the meditation with a feeling of joy and well-being.

1 Find a comfortable, upright position and gently center yourself by breathing in your own time, and draw your focus inwards so you become aware of your breath, allowing the rest of the world to fade into the background, if only for a short while.

2 Focus now on your stomach area, which can hold so much of our stress, tension, and anxiety. Allow your stomach to relax and soften. You will be in your own meditative space so you can exhale in every sense of the word and just allow any tension to dissolve.

3 As you relax, start to visualize a beautiful, golden light emanating from the stomach area; imagine this light as your healing smile, traveling through your body. Take time to create this visual and, if at first you have difficulty, simply focus on your stomach and accept whatever you receive.

4 As you visualize the light, imagine yourself as content and peaceful. See this warm glow travel up through your heart center, further filling your upper body until it reaches the top of your crown.

5 Allow the warm glow to soothe your head and face, and if you feel you are holding any tension here, just allow your jaw to relax. As you release the tension, your lips should be slightly apart.

6 Allow yourself to smile gently; the smile should feel natural and come from a place deep within. The smile doesn't have to be over-exaggerated; it is simply a smile to yourself, you are not smiling to make another person happy, this is for you. If you are finding a smile difficult, it can help to recall a time when you have felt the warm glow from meeting up with a loved one, a surprise phone call that made your day, or a message from a friend; we all get that warm, happy feeling naturally through our interaction with the people we love, but occasionally we need to integrate a visual as a reminder.

7 Sit in this meditative moment for as long as you wish and try and carry this feeling with you for the rest of the day.

To conclude: This is a useful meditation to return to when you need to give yourself a little inner comfort.

"CANDLE-GAZING" MEDITATION

The candle in this meditation acts as the focal point, which can help create a relaxing, contemplative experience. In preparation, ensure that the candle is in an appropriate holder and placed on a flat, uncluttered surface.

This meditation is best for the early evening or towards the end of the day when you are in a calmer, more reflective mood. Just ensure you keep your eyes open and stay present with the candle at all times.

1 Begin the meditation by lighting your candle and sit opposite at a safe distance—approximately one meter away—facing it at eye level. I have found that a seated position on the floor works well, with the candle placed securely on a table. As an alternative, you could also sit on a chair and place the candle on a table. Ensure that the lighting is dimmed in the room so that the candlelight is the prominent focus and all other distractions in the room simply fall away.

2 Direct your gaze to the candle's flame and simply take a moment to watch as it flickers. Notice how the flame changes shape; observe how the light in the room has softened thanks to the candle's glow.

3 As you move deeper into the meditation, allow yourself to integrate your breath work more prominently by focusing on the rise and fall of your chest. As you inhale, imagine you are breathing in the warmth of the candlelight and, as you exhale, visualize the word "calm." You can also say the word out loud if you prefer. You may want to substitute the word "calm" for another word that more closely resonates with you.

4 Continue to allow the candle to act as your focal point for the meditation and keep going for as long as you wish; this meditation can be a very relaxing exercise to carry out at the end of the day.

5 When you have come to the end of the meditation, carefully blow out the candle. This meditation is particularly helpful when you need to unwind and relax at the end of a busy day.

"I CAN'T DO THIS ALONE" MEDITATION

How many of us feel the burden of having too many things on the go and not enough hands on deck? Sometimes it can feel like we are carrying the load all by ourselves. This meditation can be carried out when you feel "full to the brim" and need to share the burden.

1 Find your meditation spot and assume a comfortable position. Spend a few seconds adjusting to the moment and gently bring your awareness to your breath. For this meditation, you can close your eyes or softly gaze just ahead of you, whatever you feel comfortable with.

2 Bring to light the issue that is causing you concern—perhaps it is something that is keeping you awake at night, leaving you feeling agitated and stressed—try not to get worked up over it, just bring the concern to the forefront in an objective, mindful way as you are taking the first steps to actually deal with this issue, which is no mean feat!

3 Imagine now that you are speaking with a loving partner, family member, friend, or perhaps even visualize yourself in this role; the most important part is that you envisage a warm, loving presence. Tell them (either aloud or in your mind) what it is that you need help with and what is troubling you most; allow yourself the opportunity to be totally honest.

4 Visualize your companion gently offering you advice and support: what would they tell you? How would they support you? What steps can they make to help you in your time of need? Just visualize the conversation so that you start to glean what you want out of a real-life discussion.

5 Imagine now that your companion is helping you make the changes you want to see in your life: imagine how much better you feel as the burden is lifted off your shoulders.

6 Gently bring your focus back to your breathing and allow yourself a few moments. You may want to bring your hand gently to your chest, which can offer comfort but also bring you back to full awareness.

To conclude: Far too often we show the people closest to us only the best part of ourselves; we plaster a smile and give "I'm fine" as a response no matter what we feel or may be going through.

we need to open up
and give our family and
friends the opportunity
to be there, and if we
become more honest
about ourselves, we are
more likely to get the
help we need when we
need it

Chapter 5

Meditations for Relationships

It is said that all relationships take work, but it's easy to forget that this "work" really does begin at home. It we are to find a fulfilling relationship, we have to come prepared with some of the groundwork already done, so we can be clear in our mind as to what we want in a partner. This way of thinking also applies to our family and friendships too; if we can bring a mindful attitude to our relationships, we can manage and sustain them through the more difficult times. When we have the willingness and intent to change what it not working for us, we then start to see positive growth. If we hide those things that are troubling us, relationships can start to fall by the wayside and resentment can set in. Meditation can help untangle the issues that have built up, so you can navigate those relationships in a clearer, more balanced frame of mind.

MINDFUL LISTENING

Mindful listening is an effective way of giving our complete attention to people and can strengthen those relationships most important to us by improving the quality and depth of the interactions we have with others.

1 Before meeting up with someone, have a few moments to yourself and bring your attention to your breathing.

2 You can start the mindful listening process by posing a few questions to yourself: when did you first get to know each other? What are the qualities that drew you to this person? Why are they special to you? This will help you glean a better understanding of the relationship you have built up over time.

3 As soon as you meet, allow the conversation to flow as it normally would, allowing your mindful approach to come to the fore gently. Begin by noticing the mood and body language of the person you are talking to, are they talking quickly or slowly? Are they happy and engaged, or perhaps quieter and more reflective than usual? Giving your full attention allows you to adapt to the conversation as it unfolds and also creates a space of understanding as you are fully aware of the other person's needs at this time.

4 As you converse, pause briefly before you form your response or answer any questions; the pause isn't for any kind of dramatic effect, it simply allows you to think about your response and choice of words, rather than talking on autopilot. In conversation with people we know well it's easy to become blasé, yet if we can be more present in what we are saying, our responses will likely be more thoughtful and considered.

5 If during the conversation you feel a strong urge to interject your opinion, just allow the impulse to pass and let whoever is speaking finish their train of thought. Respond when you have taken the time to really hear what they have said. Even a slight shift in our focus can do wonders for our social interactions.

To conclude: This level of awareness also ensures that we are mindful of other potential distractions around us. How many of us, for example, have been enjoying a perfectly nice chat with a friend or colleague only to break them off mid-sentence to answer the phone? Our concentration naturally drifts from time to time, but by allowing the other person to become the central focus, you will create a more meaningful and satisfying interaction.

WHAT DO YOU WANT IN A RELATIONSHIP?

What we look for in a relationship is a very personal matter; the one thing everyone has in common, though, is that the relationships we have encountered throughout our lives will have shown us which qualities we want and perhaps more importantly, do not want from a partner. Meditation can't conjure that perfect person, but it can give you the space to think about the qualities that are important to you in a relationship. Being clear about what we actually want will allow our energy to be focused on finding those qualities and values.

1 When using visualization in meditation, it is helpful to close your eyes so that you can start to paint a picture in your mind. Begin by visualizing a location that you are familiar with and where you spend time. The only caveat is that it needs to be somewhere social where you are likely to meet new people. It could be your local coffee shop, social group, members' club, or even the gym. Just create a visual which you are familiar with and which resonates with you.

2 As soon as you have the visual in your mind, start to imagine that you have been joined by a new acquaintance you are

just getting to know, and think about what it is like to be in their company: how does it make you feel? Are you calm or excited? Happy or nervous? Visualize the way that you would like this first meeting to go.

3 Start to move deeper into the scene: what are this person's values? Do they like similar activities as you? What are their passions? Ask questions but always keep in mind their personal values rather than your ideal aesthetic partner; if we become too wrapped up in finding a very specific look, we risk the chance of eliminating potentially great partners.

4 When you feel that you have come to the end of the meditation, bring your full attention to your breath as a way of detaching from the visualization.

To conclude: Use this exercise as a reminder of what is most important to you in a close, personal relationship.

give yourself the space
to think about what you
really want from
a relationship

PAIRED MEDITATION

Meditating together with a partner or friend can be a powerful experience and will help to strengthen the bond between you. The most important aspect of this meditation is that the intent to open the lines of communication is your shared goal. We don't possess a magic wand that will fix the issue in an instant, but with the right intention, meditation will be a step towards healing any cracks. Connecting with another person through meditation may seem unusual at first; however, if we are learning to meditate by ourselves it can be a beneficial activity to share with those closest to us.

1 To begin, find a quiet location where you can both sit comfortably. You will need to sit opposite one another, and it's important that you are both level with each other, so if you have chosen to sit on chairs, ensure that they are both the same height. Sitting on a chair is likely to be easiest and most comfortable, but if you do prefer the floor, make sure you are propped up with cushions for support.

2 If you both decide that you don't want the room to be completely silent, you can put on some relaxing background music, as long it doesn't contain lyrics that may draw your attention away from the meditation in hand.

3 When you both feel calm and ready, begin to focus on one another. Try not to overanalyze or over-think what is happening; this step helps you become familiar and comfortable with observing one another.

4 Now close your eyes, with your partner following your lead and also closing their eyes. Become aware of the sound of your own breathing and note the rise and fall of your chest. You may even detect the sound of your partner breathing—just be mindful of the present as it happens. After a few moments, signal to your partner to open their eyes, perhaps by saying "open your eyes," or by using another gesture as a gentle prompt.

5 When you are both fully aware, focus on one another again, but this time, with a thoughtful and considered approach. Notice their eyes, and start to take in other features that you have seen many times before, but probably not in as much detail. Think about the qualities that you appreciate in the other person—it is when we look deeply that we start to see the person within.

6 You may feel calm looking at your friend or partner, but you may also experience stronger emotions during this time. You cannot predict what you will feel so be gentle and understanding towards whatever comes to the surface.

7 End the session by discussing how you both felt and what your personal experiences of the meditation were.

To conclude: This exercise helps build up trust with the other person; just allowing another person to really see you is an intimate experience for friends and partners to share. The aim is to strengthen the connection between the two of you by sitting in each other's presence with a compassionate attitude. The practice can be built upon gradually as you become more comfortable doing it. You may decide to commit to five minutes at first and then progress to longer sessions if the exercise is suitable for you both.

MEDITATE WITH FRIENDS

One of the best ways to bring variety into your meditation routine is by meditating with those closest to you. It is a great way to add a new dimension to your meditative practice and can shake things up if you feel your routine is becoming a little dull and repetitive.

1 Start the conversation. It may be that meditation has never ranked particularly high on the conversation agenda. Have a chat with your friends and let them know about your interest in meditation. Suggest that you could all try a short meditative practice together.

2 Choose a venue. If you have one or two friends who are interested in trying a new activity, find a location that suits all your purposes. It may come down to who has the bigger living room, but, equally, you could pick an outdoor location such as a park or garden—the choice is up to you. You only need to have enough space for you all to sit comfortably.

3 Prepare the room. A little preparation will ensure you and your friends have an enjoyable practice. Bring in cushions, pillows, blankets, and any other props that you and your friends will need to feel comfortable.

Helpful hint

Don't be disheartened if your friends don't necessarily take to the practice in the way you had hoped. Meditation, although it can be practiced in a group setting, is a very personal experience, and so it may click for some people quite quickly while others may find they need to seek out the meditative benefits in their own way.

4 Set the scene. We are often not used to silence when in the company of friends, so you may want to put on some calming background music—this will just take the edge off the silence and help you all to settle into the experience.

5 Outline the meditation. Tell your friends the kind of meditation you will be practicing and give them a realistic time frame— you may want to suggest five minutes to begin with. I would advise carrying out the "Count the Breath" meditation (see pages 101–103), as you will be able to talk them through a detailed introduction, and then your friends can simply integrate the meditation in their own time.

6 The end of the session. As you will be taking the lead on the meditation, you will be responsible for signaling the end of the session. Place a watch directly in front of you so you can glance down after a few minutes, just to keep an eye on the time. When you feel the time has come to end the session, gently ask your friends to bring their attention back into the room. After the exercise, make sure you all have a glass of water at the ready and discuss what each one of you thought of the practice.

FOCUS ON YOUR RELATIONSHIP

Each relationship has its own set of challenges, and in the following meditation we will focus our attention on how we can successfully communicate our needs when we feel an issue has come to the surface. Sometimes we can feel unsure of how to address a problem or perhaps we are unwilling or nervous to do so. If we can simply pay attention to the issue we can start working towards finding a resolution.

1 Start by finding a comfortable place to sit and gently close your eyes. For this exercise, focus on one particular relationship in which you would like to see an improvement. Think about the relationship you currently have with this person, but rather than focusing on where you feel something is lacking, be mindful of the particular aspects that make you happy. Bringing compassion to this exercise allows us to focus on how we can make positive steps, rather than viewing the relationship from a negative angle.

2 Once you have taken some time to consider the relationship, bring your attention to your breath, which helps prevent any over-thinking. If we dwell on anything too long we may start to find fault in it, which is an unhelpful way of thinking.

3 As you settle into the meditation, gently bring your attention to one positive improvement that could strengthen and enhance your relationship. You may feel, for example, that there is a lack of real communication between the two of you; perhaps text messaging and email have taken over from face-to-face time, which can often feel alienating. This is the time to think about how you plan to discuss this matter with the other person.

4 Spend a few moments visualizing how addressing the issue you identified will start to improve your relationship. In order to become closer to people, we have to be willing to be more open about our needs.

To conclude: This visualization can help us focus on making positive steps to improve our relationships.

pay attention to issues
and work towards
a resolution

MEDITATION FOR COMPASSION

When thinking about what it means to be a compassionate person, we tend to consider how we would relate to another person who is in need of care and understanding. We rarely factor ourselves into this category. The following meditation can help you start to view yourself with greater kindness and consideration.

1 Sit in your meditation space and, as you allow yourself to relax, bring a sense of calm with you, so you are approaching this exercise from a gentle and thoughtful perspective. Your focus at this point should be on your breathing and the gentle rise and fall of your chest.

2 As you close your eyes, focus on a time in your life when you have been there for someone in need.

3 Allow this visualization to run through your mind and remember how you felt towards this person; the esteem and regard you held them in as well as the care and attention it took to make sure they were well looked after.

4 If at any time you feel emotional, come back to yourself by using the breath as a means to keep you feeling calm and in control. When we take care of our family and friends, we often don't think about the emotion and thought behind it, we just do it because we care. You might call it compassion on autopilot as we go where we are needed and do it gladly, which is why this exercise is helpful in showing us that we also need to show the same compassion to ourselves.

5 Think about how you treat yourself on a day-to-day basis and the general thought process behind this; how do you view yourself when you first wake up in the morning? If you have a hard day at work or at home, do you treat yourself kindly or are you particularly harsh and critical? If you take time out for yourself, do you feel guilty for doing this, or do you feel like you deserve time off?

6 If you have realized that you are indeed nurturing yourself, this is a wonderful affirmation, and this exercise can be used simply to remind you of the things you do to look after yourself. If, however, this has brought to light your impatience and disregard for your own well-being, now is the time to meditate on why you don't treat yourself with the same compassion you would show others.

7 When you feel ready, think about how you could now make steps towards treating yourself with the same care and respect you show for others; see yourself replacing negative thoughts with positive affirmations. Make sure that you choose something that closely relates to the situation, rather than a generic platitude. If, for example, you are having a hard day and can't get a project done on time, rather than berate yourself for this, imagine something more appropriate such as, "I have given it my best and that is all I can do. I will start afresh tomorrow." If you make yourself out to be unworthy it creates a pattern of ongoing destructive behavior. We would never want our friends and family thinking of themselves in this way, so remind yourself that you also deserve compassion. Think about working towards helping yourself in a considerate and constructive manner.

8 When you feel you have come to the end of the meditation, commit to carrying your good work forward by treating yourself with kindness and compassion in your daily life.

Chapter 6

Meditations for a Balanced Life

Leading a fulfilling life is all about seeking out new opportunities and continually challenging ourselves. If we don't seek out change, we may find an imbalance occurring, which can leave us feeling creatively unfulfilled. This is never a conducive mindset for working towards what we want to achieve. When we feel inspired, we are in a much better position to put our dreams into action, as we have the strength and the courage to follow them through. We have to constantly be aware of the dialogue that we have with ourselves so we are helping to facilitate a strong and healthy approach to life, rather than fostering a negative outlook that can very easily extinguish our creativity. These meditations will help clear away the blocks so that we can successfully balance all the aspects of our lives.

RELEASE NEGATIVE THOUGHTS

In order to maintain a balanced and positive outlook on life, we need to curb negative thinking. We all have, at times, found ourselves with a trail of unhelpful thoughts as we go about our day. These thoughts can range from worrying over a deadline to not having enough time to meet friends, job performance, or general feelings of frustration...The list can seem endless. We also tend to dwell on these thoughts, so they ultimately become an all-consuming presence in our lives. The following meditation can be useful when we need to readdress the negative balance.

1 Find a comfortable spot in your home where you can sit for this meditation. Begin by bringing your awareness to your breath as this will help you to relax and focus on the meditation. You can gently close your eyes.

2 Focus on a particular thought that you have recently been dwelling on and that has distracted and clouded your thinking. Just allow the thought to run through your mind as you build a picture of what has been worrying you. Try not to get involved with the thought on an emotional level, instead become the observer of your thought, as if it is running through your mind like a mini-movie; this can help you to see the problem in a more objective light.

3 Now think what your normal response would be to the issue that you are thinking about. What happens when you feel upset? Do you get angry, passive-aggressive, or maybe you just walk away? Spend a few moments considering and understanding your usual reaction.

4 For this next step, keep the issue that has been troubling you at the forefront, but this time see yourself handling the situation in a constructive and pragmatic way that enables you to remain balanced and in control. Think about the words you would use and the steps you would take to deal with the situation head on. How does it now feel to go about your day without the baggage that comes with continual over-thinking? What have you gained from releasing this negativity? What is your mindset like once you relinquish the need to hold on to negative thoughts?

5 When you feel you have come to the end of the meditation, bring your awareness back to the breath and gently open your eyes.

To conclude: This meditation can be used as often as you like. It works as a helpful reminder to maintain a positive and balanced mindset.

Once we make the decision to tackle our negative thoughts, it allows us to rein in our over-thinking and replace habitual negativity with thoughts that are more conducive to happiness and creativity.

to maintain a balanced
and positive outlook,
we need to curb
negative thinking

FIND YOUR PATH

In order to feel more fulfilled in our lives, we need to find out what makes us happy and what it is that gives us that surge of excitement. The trouble is, finding out what we really want can also be rather difficult, as the thing we are looking for may seem intangible at times; we can sense that there is something more but we can't always put our finger on precisely what that is. Meditation can be used as a kind of sounding board to play around with ideas, dreams, and aspirations; your very own space to start building towards your goals.

1 Find a comfortable place to sit. For this exercise, you can close your eyes or keep them open, just as long as you pick a specific point in the room on which to focus. Ask yourself the question: "What is it I want to do?" You don't have to analyze it or think about it in great detail, just throw it out into the room. It can help to ask the question aloud.

2 Bring your attention to your breathing and allow yourself to ruminate gently on the question you have asked, without thinking too hard or wracking your brain for an answer. Just trust what comes up (even if at this moment you have drawn a blank) and remain firmly in the moment by keeping your breath as the point of focus. If we allow ourselves to be relaxed and open we encourage inspiration to strike.

3 The answer may come up unexpectedly or further into the meditation. Try not to feel that the answer has to be perfectly in line with what you were hoping for; it doesn't have to be something on a grand scale, like your ultimate career objective, instead it could be something more immediate, such as deciding that you would like to go traveling. It's good to remember that what we want is always changing and evolving, so don't be concerned if you find that your goals and objectives are different from what you originally thought.

4 When the answer comes to the fore, ask yourself why you haven't yet made strides towards achieving this objective; it may be due to financial reasons, time constraints, or perhaps you simply haven't given it much thought. Now is the time to think about what you could do to move towards realizing this goal for yourself.

5 The next step is to visualize achieving this objective; how do you feel now? Is there a sense of satisfaction? Do you feel content, exhilarated, relieved? If we get a sense of what the reality could potentially feel like, it then begins to take shape as an idea; visualization is that first step to realizing what it is we want.

6 This exercise can be used any time you decide you want to make a change, to help you ascertain what is most important to you right now.

To conclude: Our path doesn't have to follow a set structure and can change to accommodate our needs. If we think about what we truly want for ourselves we will likely come up with one or two ideas that we have not previously considered. This meditation will help you to clarify both your immediate goals and your dreams for the future.

SIMPLIFY YOUR LIFE

Day-to-day life can be made immeasurably easier when we cut back and make more use of those items that truly have value to us. If we think about the items we are continually drawn to, they are likely to have deeper meaning for us, or they are necessary for day-to-day living. Yet, we often find that superfluous items we probably don't remember purchasing or receiving have invaded our personal space. The following exercise will help you ask yourself the ultimate consumer question: do I really need this?

1 Find the room in your home where you tend to store most of your purchases and unused gifts. You may have a closet or drawer where, along with your clothes, you have stowed away items for when they might come in useful. Spend a few moments, sitting wherever is comfortable with your feet planted firmly on the ground, and bring your attention to your breath.

2 Think about the items you see in this room and how many times you have used them. Are they of value to you? Have they been worth the cost? Are the items worth the space they currently take up in your home? I know we don't often pay this much attention to inanimate things, but when we start to focus on what we want and choose to surround ourselves with, we can see with clarity the items that have surreptitiously encroached on our personal space.

3 Now focus on one item in particular and meditate on the following questions: Would you miss the item if you didn't have it? Is it something you get regular use out of? By asking simple questions you start to get a picture of the value that you have placed on the item. If you have come back with a resounding "yes" to both questions, they clearly have value to you and are worth keeping.

To conclude:
Next time you go shopping, just take a moment to ask yourself whether the item you covet will be of use to you and whether it would add value to your life. The exercise simply brings to light what it is that works for us, so that we can have the things we want and need.

LOOK TO THE FUTURE

This particular meditation enables us to start to plan for things
to come, to visualize and help create our future, giving us
clarity in understanding our goals, all the while remaining
grounded in the here and now. For this exercise, you will
need a notepad and a pen.

1 Get comfortable in your meditation area, gently close your
eyes, and find your center by breathing gently, keeping your
focus on the rise and fall of your chest. Focus on your breath for
as long as you wish as this helps to calm and balance you
before the visualization.

2 Allow yourself to be calm and,
when you feel ready, in your
own time, gently open your
eyes, place the notepad on
your lap, and write down
your hopes and dreams for the
future. They don't have to be in
chronological order or have any
specific correlation, just write down
ideas, phrases, or even feelings,
which relate to what you hope to

achieve. You can scrawl over the page in large letters, small letters, or even use illustrations if you are feeling particularly creative; it should be your thoughts and feelings, uninhibited by your impulse to dilute your dreams in any way. This is not the time for modest thinking—really state your dreams with clarity and intent. Remember, this sheet of paper is for your eyes only.

3 Once you have filled the paper with your ideas and musings, spend the next few minutes simply looking over the page to get a sense of what you are pulled towards and what ideas and thoughts jump off the page; what is the dream you yearn for the most? Choose the one that you are drawn to, not the dream you think you ought to pick.

4 Close your eyes to return to the meditation. Focus on your breath and then, after a few moments, bring your chosen goal to the fore in your mind. Ask yourself a few questions in order to gain clarity on what it is you wish to achieve:

Why have I chosen this particular ambition?

What would it mean to my life if I achieved it?

What are the steps I now need to take to get there?

You don't have to answer all the questions in this one meditation session. This exercise could even be carried out over the course of a week, in which you give yourself the time to work through the questions.

5 Once you have asked yourself the questions, simply allow yourself to ruminate on those thoughts at your own pace. You might like to refocus on your breath and then, if an idea or thought comes up, make a note of it. Try not to analyze the thoughts or feelings, even if you think they appear silly or overambitious; whatever may come up, just allow it to evolve organically. Remember, everything that has ever been achieved started with an idea, so allow yourself the same time to think and create.

6 When you feel that you have come to the end of the meditation, sit quietly for a few moments. This allows the information to assimilate and you can look back on your notes later with fresh eyes.

To conclude: Practice this meditation when you want help visualizing your goals and objectives.

REACH YOUR POTENTIAL

It's easy to put a cap on our own abilities, believe we are only proficient in one area, or view our abilities as finite. When we put a limit on ourselves, it immediately shrinks our potential and stops us from taking chances. The following exercise can help you to address any long-held beliefs you have about yourself that may be limiting your potential.

For this meditation, you will be observing your own reflection and you can sit or stand in front of a mirror. To improve our belief in our own potential, we have to deal with the very person who is placing limits on what we feel we can achieve—our own self.

1 While standing or sitting in front of a mirror, take a few moments to center yourself so you feel calm and focused. Look at yourself in the mirror, not in the superficial way we often regard ourselves (noticing a hair out of place, observing a line, or fretting over a particular feature); but the self you are looking at is the you that strives, achieves, struggles, sometimes disappoints, loves, laughs…Think of all you have been through and the strength it has taken over the years to get to where you are today, and now look at yourself through these eyes.

2 Focus on a particular long-held belief you have about yourself, whether you think you can't communicate what you want and need or feel afraid to take the next step.

3 Ask yourself what it is that is holding you back. Be honest here; this meditation is just for you, so there is no reason to

contrive an answer. Once we acknowledge our worries and concerns, we can then choose either to live with them or take the necessary steps to change things. Make a commitment to yourself to start making small steps towards changing this limiting belief. If, for example, you feel worried about asking for what you want in your work life, commit to beginning to tackle this situation, which may mean simply opening up to those around you so they know your needs and can give you the necessary support to start making those changes.

4 You can finish the meditation with a positive affirmation that, when spoken with intent and conviction, can help you reiterate to yourself what it is you really want and empower you to believe you can achieve it. Just remember to keep the affirmation positive and confident; you have to feel you are already living what you want so, for example, you could say: "I am working toward and achieving my goals" rather than "I hope to" or "I would like to."

To conclude: This meditation can be used whenever you need a confidence boost. Remember to look at your reflection with compassion at all times, making sure that the affirmation is positive and encouraging.

Chapter 7

Meditations on the Go

It is often assumed that meditation requires a cross-legged position and complete stillness in order to reap its benefits successfully, which is simply not the case. You can meditate even while on the go, which means you are unrestricted in how you choose to practice; it instantly opens up what we think of as meditation, as we can get our mindful, meditative moments wherever we happen to be. So, whether you are carrying out the daily chores, working out at the gym, or commuting on the train to work, you will find the right exercise for you.

WASHING THE DISHES

We tend to do our daily chores without much thought or consideration; we're merely going through the motions. Of course, simply applying mindfulness won't suddenly transform these tasks into the sunny centerpieces of the day, but if we can choose to be present in our daily tasks, we may be able to find a little more satisfaction in those "to dos" that are such a prominent part of daily life.

Modern technology is a wonderful thing and for those with a dishwasher, this time-consuming chore can be carried out with the mere flick of a switch. Yet there will always be a certain amount of manual labor involved; someone has the not-so-glamorous job of loading the dishwasher, after all.

The following exercise can be carried out in two ways: if you are dishwasher-free, fill up the basin as you normally would. However, if you have a dishwasher, see Step 5, showing that you can also incorporate mindfulness for this activity.

1 Once you are at the kitchen basin, take a moment to be still and become aware of your breathing. The act of stilling the body and quieting the mind helps signify that this won't be an entirely normal dishwashing session.

2 Every action you take needs your full co-operation and consideration, as if you were carrying out a favorable activity in which you want to savor each moment. The act of mindfulness requires you to be open to what naturally occurs as you carry out the task.

3 Turn the faucet on and watch as the water fills the basin; notice how the water froths as it reacts with the detergent, clouding almost instantly. Take your first item, place it in the basin, and, as you clean, become closely aware of the action involved. Watch how the item is immersed, think about your skin making contact with the water, you can even hold the item up to the light and notice how it appears once it has been scrubbed clean.

4 Be mindful of how you place your items on the draining board and be aware of how long it has taken to scrub, rinse, and stack the dishes.

5 If you have a dishwasher, this mindful task can be carried out as you load and unload the machine, taking care as you restock your cabinets, placing the items in their rightful home.

6 When you have finished, take a look at your kitchen and allow yourself to feel that sense of satisfaction that comes from completing a task.

To conclude: This exercise can be carried out anytime you want to bring a mindful approach to life's daily chores. By giving our full attention to the process, we give ourselves a break from the constant stream of internal chatter as we immerse ourselves in the task at hand.

ON THE MOVE

It's a perfectly clear, crisp
day and ripe for a walk.
I love days like this because
they are the optimum and
beneficial time for applying
mindfulness. Wherever you
happen to live, exploring the
places we know and love can
be an interesting way of turning
our attention to what is
already around us.

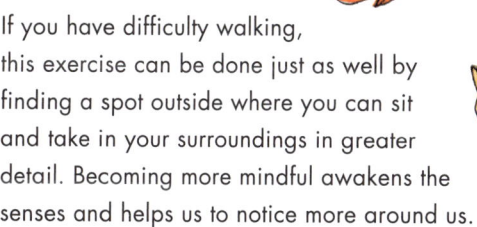

If you have difficulty walking,
this exercise can be done just as well by
finding a spot outside where you can sit
and take in your surroundings in greater
detail. Becoming more mindful awakens the
senses and helps us to notice more around us.
How many times, for example, have you stopped in your
tracks to answer your cellphone and, as you look around, your
gaze lands on something you hadn't noticed before, even
though you might have passed by that spot every day? You
can, however, make time for yourself, so you don't miss what
is right in front of you.

1 Start the exercise mindfully by preparing for your walk; bring your focus to the preliminary activity of pulling on your boots or zipping up a jacket to help set yourself in the right frame of mind.

2 As you leave your home, bring your attention to the activity in hand. It is likely you will be carrying your cellphone, and I realize that this is a necessity for most people, but if you can turn it off temporarily, all the better. You could always let your loved ones know that you won't be available for the next 30 minutes, or however long you plan to be, so that they have peace of mind. Alternatively, just switch your cellphone to silent so that you can check in if you need to.

3 As you set off on your walk, keep your pace even and steady.

4 As you walk, think about how your body feels and the impact of each step: Are you balanced and in control? What terrain are you walking on? Are you on a flat surface, stones, grass? Think about what you are experiencing underfoot, not just your location.

5 Halfway through your walk, sit down and take in a more stationary perspective; this will give you the opportunity not only to refuel, but to take stock of your surroundings.

6 As you continue on the move you will also find yourself having to interact with other people, such as minding your step or stopping and starting to allow people to pass. Although we may be taking our time to walk with consideration, many others will not, so don't let them be a distraction. These need not be obstacles to your mindful walking, but can be integrated into the experience.

7 When you arrive home and have come to the end of your mindful walking, take a moment to think about what you experienced. You will likely be surprised to find that you remember your walk with much more clarity and in more detail than usual.

To conclude: Walking with a greater sense of presence can help us to enjoy something as simple as getting out of the house; it becomes a richer, more rewarding activity. To add variety to this exercise, walk in various different locations to help keep yourself interested.

OUTDOOR MEDITATION

Your meditation ritual can
be taken outside with a few
simple adjustments to your
usual meditation spot. If you have
a garden or are close to a local park, meditation can be
adapted to bring nature into your practice.

1 Find a quiet location in your garden or local park. For this
meditation, you simply need to use the sounds and smells
around you; this acts as your point of focus and helps you
appreciate your surroundings.

2 Find a comfortable place to sit and gently close your eyes.
Begin by taking some calming, soothing breaths. Spend a few
moments noticing the rise and fall of your chest as you breathe.

3 Start to expand your focus to what you can hear around you:
can you discern people chatting in the near distance? Perhaps
you can hear birds as they flit between branches or the rustling of
leaves? You may even hear the low hum of cars in the distance.
Simply allow what you are hearing to come gently into focus. Try
not to let your focus simply land on the most pleasant sound; allow
whatever is happening around you to become clear in your mind.

4 Now bring your focus to the smells around you: perhaps you have picked up on freshly cut grass, or maybe you are near a flower bed so you can detect its perfume. If you happen to be in a park, a food cart may be nearby, so be present to the cooking aromas and the hive of activity that may be in your vicinity. Meditating outside can be a feast for the senses.

5 Once you feel you have honed in on the sounds and smells around you, gently open your eyes and take the time to appreciate what is in front of you. Calmly connect with what you have just experienced; really see what is around you.

To conclude: Meditating outdoors helps you reconnect to your surroundings, and it's also beneficial during the warmer seasons when you want to be outside enjoying the weather.

THE MINDFUL SWEEP

There is something about the act of sweeping that can be extremely satisfying. I think it must be connected with getting things back to the way they should be: clean, uncluttered, and simple. You can apply mindfulness when sweeping the floors at home to practice focusing on a single task.

1 Find a place in your home where you can sweep, it may be your hall or kitchen, for example. Spend a few moments just observing your surroundings and noticing where you will need to start.

2 Choose a corner in which to start and begin methodically, progressively working your way around the floor space, following the bristles as they collect dust and dirt. Observe how you move with the broom, being mindful of how you are working, and the energy and effort it takes.

3 If you find you need to take a break during this exercise, rather than head to another room to start another task, just take a seat where you are, or stand if it is easier, and be observant of the progress you have already made. Try not to get distracted by any other household chores you might have noticed, and keep with what you are doing; notice where you have cleaned and where else in the room you need to focus on.

4 Once you feel the floor has been swept successfully, spend a few moments listening to the sound of your breath and be aware of how you feel post-activity.

5 You can now apply this mindful approach to the next item on your to-do list.

To conclude: Approaching a simple household chore with mindfulness can help bring a sense of satisfaction and completion to a simple day-to-day activity.

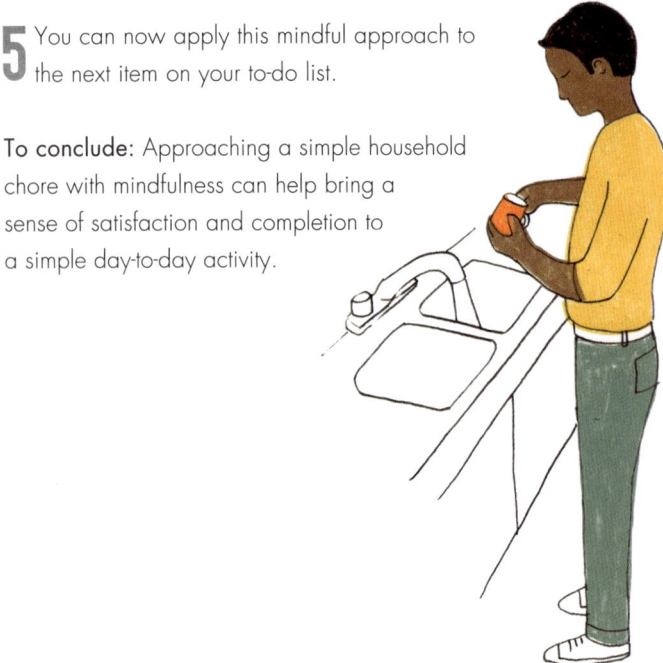

GYM MEDITATION

If there wasn't already enough evidence to convince you of the benefits of a healthy lifestyle, this next meditation is doubly convincing, providing a mental and physical workout. The beauty of the gym is that it provides a structured setting where we are less likely to slack off, so it can be the ideal place to carry out a mindfulness practice. This exercise works particularly well on the treadmill, but could equally be used on an exercise bike or other stationary exercise equipment.

This meditation can be carried out for the duration of your workout session. For example, if you usually use the treadmill for 15 minutes, this could be your time frame.

1 Set about your walk or run as you normally would, but rather than paying attention to the music in the background or the television on the wall ahead, keep your focus on your breathing and be aware of any changes as you increase your pace on the treadmill.

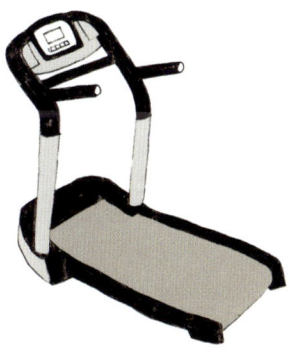

2 Bring your mindfulness practice to the fore and become more aware of your body as you work it; think about the effort that is required as you adjust the incline or pace. For this step, use the same practice as in the "Body Scan Meditation" in chapter 4 (see pages 107–109). Starting with your feet, working up through the legs, torso, your shoulders and neck, until you reach the top of your crown, become closely aware of what you are experiencing in your body as you exercise. When we notice this level of detail we can cultivate more of an appreciation for how hard our body works and the level of effort required to carry out an activity. This can also bring a sense of satisfaction in what we have achieved, which can often be taken for granted.

3 If you find at any time that your attention has wandered, or you feel you are drifting off into your own thoughts, bring yourself back to the exercise with your breath as the focus.

4 Once you have finished the exercise, take a moment to ground yourself and feel how your body responds as you begin the cool down.

To conclude: By incorporating mindfulness into your gym session, you will develop a greater appreciation for your workout and you will also have a new, more thoughtful perspective on your fitness routine.

MINDFUL SHOPPING

It's an activity we all have to do at some point, whether buying for ourselves or shopping for gifts for family and friends, for many people it can be one of the more stressful of recreational pursuits. It is of course far easier now with online shopping being only a few clicks away, but we will, on occasion, find ourselves having to navigate the busy shopping streets. The most important aspect of a shopping excursion has to be "awareness," as this can offset any potential concerns when you have a clear and defined shopping structure.

We often become scattered in our thinking when shopping as we are presented with such a vast array of choice; it is, you could say, the perfect distraction. How many of us, for example, have gone on a busy shopping trip only to come home and wonder what we have actually purchased? We might not have even remembered buying the items or indeed noticed the price. If we are mindful and present when we are shopping, we can make informed and balanced decisions. This exercise is an extension of the meditation "Simplify Your Life" in chapter 6 (see pages 149–150).

1 Before you leave your home, I would suggest integrating a short breath-meditation exercise (see pages 48–49) just to help you feel balanced and centered before you head out.
This will help you to feel calmer, and more focused before the shopping trip.

2 As soon as you are ready to leave, ensure that you have prepared a written shopping list so it can help you keep track of what you need to purchase and, perhaps more importantly, what you don't need.

3 As you make your way to the shops, be mindful of your every step and allow this activity to become your central focus. Notice your presence as you walk along the street and be conscious of the breath. This also helps you stay more in control and makes it less likely to throw you off balance by the flow of shoppers as they rush past. In busy shopping centers, it is easy to just follow the crowd and head into the store that is positively bustling with activity. If we can keep on course, and are fully aware of what we are doing, we are less likely to be seduced into mindless purchasing.

4 When you head into a shop, immediately walk towards the department where you need to make your purchase. It is often tempting to relinquish the "to-do" list for the more pleasurable, list-free shopping, of course.

5 If you find yourself picking up an additional item not on your shopping list, just pause for a moment and think about why you need it. There will always be the rush that comes with having something "new," but if you are aware of how quickly this impulse passes, you will be in a better frame of mind to make an informed decision.

To conclude: Mindful shopping doesn't necessarily mean you can't treat yourself, it simply helps curb the tendency for overspending. When we become mindful of our purchases, we are also showing respect for ourselves by discerning what is right for us at any given time.

It's the smart, mindful shopper that ultimately gets the most consumer satisfaction.

THE MINDFUL COMMUTER

Making our way from A to B may sound simple, but a daily commute can often take its toll on our well-being. If we are lucky enough not to have to take transportation to our place of work, we can count ourselves fortunate indeed. The issue we all experience with commuting is that it is a tiresome activity, often lengthy in duration, and your personal space is likely to be taken up by fellow commuters. It's never going to be a relaxing journey, but it can be given a mindful overhaul so you can integrate a worthwhile activity while getting to your chosen destination.

On the train, I often notice people reading a book, magazine, or listening to their music, and all these activities have their own meditative benefits. However, if you find yourself without anything to occupy your time, I suggest the following mindful exercise, which is ideal if you are traveling on public transport.

1 In your current position, whether you happen to be sitting or standing, try and find that moment of personal calm by focusing on your breath. As it is likely to be noisy on the train, bus, or subway, you may not even be able to detect your breath, so focus on what you can pick up on. Can you feel the air as it touches the tip of your nostrils? Or maybe you are following the rise and fall of your chest? Spend a few moments finding your rhythm in order to help you feel more calm and centered.

2 After a few minutes of focusing on your breathing, expand your awareness to where you currently are in your space and become mindful of how your body is positioned. This exercise is all about becoming more aware of "you." When we commute, we are often swept along with the other passengers, and sometimes it feels as if we're just following the crowd. But if you can bring your "self" into clearer focus, you will become more mindful of your journey, so you will be kinder to yourself, and equally more conscious and considerate of your fellow commuters.

To conclude: This exercise can be carried out for the duration of your commute, or you may decide to practice for five minutes and then carry on reading your book or listening to music. You can mix and match this exercise to fit your needs on any given day.

MEDITATE AT YOUR DESK

During busy work periods, you may often find yourself a permanent fixture at your desk, working from morning until late at night, barely pausing for breath—sound familiar? You may have found that during your working hours you very rarely look up from your screen, in fact, you may take no breaks at all. The following meditation will encourage you to take more mindful breaks throughout your working day.

1 In your seated position at your desk, take a break from work whether you are currently typing on the computer or making notes in your diary. Take a moment to become still and aware of your breathing. You can place your hands on the desk in front of you or just rest them on your knees.

2 For this exercise, keep your eyes open as this meditation is all about observing and being aware of the moment.

3 Rest your gaze on an item currently on your desk, it could be your cellphone, laptop, a pen, or even a notepad—allow this to become your central focus.

4 If you have honed in on your cellphone, for example, take a moment to think about what this item means to you: how much time do you spend on your phone? How does it assist you in your daily life? Do you feel it enhances your life? You may choose to consider all these questions, however, it may be more conducive just to pick out one of the questions and focus on that particular thought. Try not to get emotionally involved, simply think about this item that you use day in, day out, and how it has become part of your life. This can help you to evaluate how much you rely on this item; perhaps you have realised that you need to cut back, or it may have highlighted how much this technology helps you in your day-to day life—sometimes it's simply a case of finding a healthy balance between the two.

5 If at any time you feel distracted, or perhaps you hear some chatter from colleagues or noise outside, allow this to become part of the exercise and try not to feel agitated by the external activity—your breathing is the anchor that keeps you centered and in the present moment.

6 You may have also picked up on low buzzing from your computer—allow this to come into your realm of focus.

7 The next step is to remove your focus from your first item to another object that happens to catch your eye. This also keeps the exercise interesting as you can draw your attention to as many items as you choose: allow yourself to ask the same questions you did with the first item.

To conclude: This exercise can be included whenever you feel your working life is chaotic. Sometimes we all need to take stock of how we are spending our days so that we can work towards getting that perfect work-life balance.

COFFEE-BREAK EXERCISE

When you next take a break to make a hot drink for yourself, a friend, or a colleague, take this opportunity to be mindful.

1 As you begin to make the drink, be aware and involved in every step. As you reach for the cup, fill the kettle,

place the bag in the cup, or spoon the coffee in the cafetière—whatever action is required—give each step your full, undivided attention. Be present with the weight of the cup as you take it from the cupboard, take in the aroma of the coffee, or observe how the tea bag infuses in the cup as you pour the hot water. Allow these actions to be your sole focus and priority for this moment, rather than feeling distracted by the next item on your to-do list.

2 When you sit down to take a sip of the drink, enjoy what you have just made for yourself. Think about the taste, the temperature, and how you feel as you drink your beverage.

To conclude: This activity can be integrated to help make the most of your break time. We often make a drink for ourselves with a cellphone attached to one ear, or, we may be talking with another person in the room, all the while switched onto autopilot while preparing the drink. If we can better discern those opportunities in the day where we can take full advantage and utilize the time for mindfulness, we will feel more refreshed and ready for the next item on the agenda.

Conclusion

Continuing the good work

The first couple of months of any new activity are always the "honeymoon" period. It occupies more of your time than anything else and may have your friends and family wondering why. Though meditation is an understated activity, and probably not likely to monopolize your every waking thought, like any new endeavor that has caught our attention, it can very quickly become yesterday's news. Below are some suggestions on how meditation can withstand the initial infatuation period to become something that is workable within your daily schedule.

To begin, it is best to make a plan of what can realistically be fitted into your life and to think about what your schedule entails. Write down what your typical week consists of and note where you feel you could factor in your meditation time. As with the changing nature of schedules, your week's agenda could suddenly shift and what you thought you could manage might now seem impossible, which is why you should always be flexible. If you work long hours and your job is highly stressful, think about those times when you do eventually relax, whether you unwind by watching television or reading a book, just assign ten minutes out of your relaxation time to your meditation practice.

FURTHER TIPS FOR STAYING MOTIVATED

Timely and to the point: It is always best to keep the timings short and relevant to you, as has been suggested throughout. You may find, for example, that meditating while out and about lends itself to a specific time frame, such as your commute to the office. If during the course of this book, you have found that particularly short time frames such as a few minutes are all you need, keep with that. On paper it looks incredibly speedy, but mere minutes can make all the difference, and short practices can certainly be a good way of remaining motivated.

Keep a progress diary: It is so easy to forget how far we have come when our focus is so often on where we feel we haven't progressed. The best way to keep track of your meditation sessions is to make a note in your diary or journal, with enough information for you to be able to look back on each session in the weeks and months to come. Make a note of the time when you practice and the length of the session, as well as your thoughts on the meditation itself such as whether you felt relaxed, calm, and fully in the moment, or restless and slightly agitated.

From this information, you will start to recognize patterns and see those times when you are clearly reaping the benefits, as well as notice when the practice hasn't felt as productive. You may find, for example, that you always feel restless when you meditate straight after work, because you're conscious of the other things you have to do that evening. Work with this information and alter your routine accordingly.

It's for comfort—not the catwalk: When meditating, it's best to dress for comfort, so the less restrictive the clothing, the better—comfortable trousers, t-shirts, and jumpers. It's never going to be a glamorous affair, but it is one of those blissful times in the day when you can relax; the time is just for you, after all. Of course, this is slightly different when we are meditating "on the go" and are likely to be wearing a more formal outfit if we are heading to our place of work, but if you do happen to be in the comfort of your own home, dress in the way that is most comfortable and conducive to your meditation practice.

And breathe

This book can now be used alongside your meditation practice, any time you feel you need to refresh your routine and to source new ideas. The key is to keep your meditation practice relevant to your lifestyle.

Do bear in mind that there is no fixed endpoint to meditation. If you are following an exercise regime, the goal may be to reach a target weight or, if you participate in a competitive sport, your aim may be to score as many points as you can. With meditation, there is no set goal and the objective is simply to be with yourself on a continual basis. Meditation is a way of approaching life and your "meditation muscle" will get stronger the more you use it and invest in yourself.

Meditation has always been used to assist in understanding the self, to help re-evaluate long-held beliefs about ourselves, to challenge negative thought processes, to re-examine the things in life we feel most passionate about, and to be more present in our own lives. The practice itself is subtle, yet it can be an incredibly enriching and rewarding experience. I hope that you enjoy discovering the practice for yourself and integrating it into your life in your own unique way.

Index

References

Page 12: Suzuki, S., *Zen Mind, Beginner's Mind*, (Shambhala, 2011).

Page 32: Jacobs, T.L. et al., "Self-Reported Mindfulness and Cortisol Control During a Shamatha Meditation Retreat", *Health Psychology*, vol. 32 (10, 2013), pp 1104—1109.

Acknowledgments

Bringing a book together is a collaborative effort and I would like to thank all the people involved and, in particular, Lauren Mulholland, who guided me through every step of the editorial process, and for being such a wonderful source of support. I would also like to thank Cindy Richards, Elanor Clarke, Jennifer Jahn, Vanessa Bird, Sally Powell, Emily Breen, Rosie Scott, Melissa Launay, Gordana Simakovic, Meskerem Berhane, Mark McGinlay, and Kerry Lewis. I am also very grateful to Tonya L. Jacobs who kindly answered my questions. I was lucky enough to be represented by the best—Diane Banks Associates—and want to thank Olivia Morris who negotiated the deal for me. I am also brilliantly encouraged by my Mum and Dad, who have championed my work from the beginning. And a very special thank you to John Wright who has, over the years, been my ideas man/editor/proofreader/advice-giver and, now, husband.